THE

FOR SALE BY OWNER

KIT

SECOND EDITION

▶ **ATTRACTING THE BUYER**

▶ **CLOSING THE DEAL**

▶ **SAVING $$$ ON COMMISSIONS**

ROBERT IRWIN

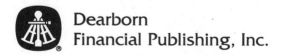
Dearborn
Financial Publishing, Inc.

This publication is designed to provide accurate and authoritative information in regard to the subject matter covered. It is sold with the understanding that the publisher is not engaged in rendering legal, accounting or other professional service. If legal advice or other expert assistance is required, the services of a competent professional person should be sought.

Acquisitions Editor: Christine Litavsky
Managing Editor: Jack Kiburz
Associate Project Editor: Stephanie C. Schmidt
Interior Design: Lucy Jenkins
Cover Design: S. Laird Jenkins Corporation

© 1993 and 1996 by Dearborn Financial Publishing, Inc.®

Published by Dearborn Financial Publishing, Inc.®

Printed in the United States of America.

96 97 98 10 9 8 7 6 5 4 3 2 1

Library of Congress Cataloging-in-Publication Data

Irwin, Robert, 1941–
    The for sale by owner kit / Robert Irwin.–2nd ed.
        p.   cm.
    Includes index.
    ISBN 0-7931-1529-9 (pbk.)
    1. House selling–Handbooks, manuals, etc. 2. House selling–
United States–Handbooks, manuals, etc. I. Title.
HD1379.I644   1995   95-4707
333.33'8–dc20   CIP

Contents

CHAPTER
ONE

Getting Up the Nerve

You *can* sell your home by owner. People from all walks of life and backgrounds, some with little knowledge of real estate, do it every day in all parts of the country. (Estimates show that in some states as many as 20 percent of all sales are handled by owners.) The real question, of course, is not can you do it, but can you do it easily, quickly and correctly?

There are lots of fears and concerns, some justified, some not, among homeowners who are considering selling on their own. Here are just a few of the negative arguments that I've heard. Are some of these yours?

- I can't understand the paperwork.
- I'm no good at selling.
- I wouldn't even know where to begin!
- I don't have the time.
- It's just too hard.
- It's dangerous to invite strangers into your house.

Maybe you've heard other reasons not to sell your home on your own, but I think these pretty much detail their scope. Basically they are: "I don't know how" and "I'm afraid."

You *Can* Do It

If you want to sell your home as an owner by yourself, you can do it. For every argument against, there are solid reasons why it will work. Let's consider the six concerns noted above:

1. *Paperwork*—You can *always* find someone else to do the paperwork for you. I don't mean they'll do it for free (although a competent friend might); I mean that you can pay them a reasonable set fee and they'll handle it. On the East Coast there are some attorneys who do nothing else. On the West Coast and elsewhere some real estate brokers make extra money this way. We'll see how to get someone else to do the paperwork in Chapter 6.

2. *Salesmanship*—While there are some who seem to be "born" salespeople, I suspect that most of us feel awkward or embarrassed by having to sell something. We feel we could never pressure someone into buying our house. The truth, however, is that good salespeople don't use pressure. They simply present the product (in this case a house) in the best light and let the buyers sell themselves.

   Now, who is more qualified to extol the virtues of your own property than you? We'll go into all sorts of sales tips in Chapter 7.

3. *Where to begin*—That's easy. All you need is curiosity and a healthy desire to save time and money. You'll be surprised what motivators these are! In Chapter 3 we'll discuss a quick sales plan anyone can use to get started turning that house around right now.

4. *Time*—Most people think that selling by owner means spending *more* time. Actually, if you do it right, you can *save* time in most markets. That's right, a FSBO can move quicker than a listed property. (By the way, the term *FSBO,* pronounced fizzbo, is an acronym for For Sale By

Owner, the title of this book.) In Chapter 5 we'll see how proper pricing can produce a quicker sale.

5. *Too hard*—It's all a matter of perspective. How hard is it not to sell at all? How hard is it to pay a huge commission to an agent? Going through the hoops required to sell by yourself can seem downright easy when compared to those two big "hardnesses."

6. *Strangers*—No one likes strangers in his house. But let's face it, no matter which way you sell, you're going to have to let strangers see the place. If you do it yourself, you can minimize the risk by showing the property only at reasonable hours, only after having qualifying the prospective buyers on the phone, and by having someone you for the appointment. More safety tips are in Chapter 7.

Why You Should Sell Your Home by Yourself

As you see, there are reasonable ways to get around most objections to selling a home "by owner." Plus, there are a number of solid advantages to doing so. Here are four that I think are excellent.

1. It Can Save You Money

Quite frankly, the reason most people want to sell FSBO is to save the amount they would have to pay on a commission to an agent. While real estate commissions are fully negotiable between seller and agent, my experience has been that most run between 5 and 7 percent of the sales price. If we take 6 percent as an average, that means that on a $100,000 house, the commission is $6,000. On a $250,000 house, it's $15,000. That's a lot of money to save.

Please note, I'm not saying that agents charge too much. Those in the field know that good ones work hard and earn every penny. I am simply saying that it's a lot of money to spend if you're a seller, particularly if you can avoid it by doing the work yourself.

2. *It Can Preserve Your Equity*

While a commission is based on the selling price, it's paid out of your equity in the home. While a $6,000 commission may only be 6 percent of a $100,000 sales price, if your equity in the property is only $20,000, the commission is actually 30 percent of equity. By selling by owner, you can preserve your equity.

3. *It Can Get You a Quicker Sale*

While most people want to save money by selling by owner, many others simply want a quicker sale. They want to get out of the property as rapidly as possible. One way to do this is to give, in effect, an amount equal to all (or a portion) of the commission to the buyer. If all the homes like yours are selling for $150,000, instead of listing at that price and paying, for example, a $9,000 commission, simply sell by owner and reduce the price by $9,000 (or less). Suddenly, your home can be 5, 6, even 7 percent below market. Instead of paying a commission to an agent, you're paying an equal amount to the buyer.

It comes out the same to you. However, price-sensitive buyers will swarm to your door for this bargain.

4. *It Can Get You Started in a New Method of Investing*

Many very well-off real estate investors of today got their start by selling their homes on their own years ago. It taught them how real estate deals are handled. And nothing builds confidence and knowledge more than successfully selling by yourself. Real estate investing careers have to start someplace and doing a FSBO is a great way in.

It's Not Quite That Simple

Before you get the impression that selling a home is as easy as falling off a log, rest assured, it's not. If it were, there wouldn't be any agents. Everyone would simply sell their own homes.

Given all the positive reasons to sell by owner, the vast majority of people still fail to do so. A reasonable person has to ask, why do so many people bypass this alternative and directly list their homes?

First, there's simply the matter of nerve. While few of us would hesitate to have a garage sale to sell almost anything from used clothing to an old piano, or put an ad in the paper to sell the family car, most of us are nonetheless intimidated by the apparently daunting task of selling our own homes. Most people would be happy to conduct the sale of just about any item you can think of by themselves, except their houses. Let's face it, you have to be just a little bit gutsy to sell by owner.

But don't let a failure of nerve stop you from selling FSBO. Remember, it is possible to acquire all the techniques and abilities you fear you don't possess. You can get a buyer to sign a sales agreement. You can learn to handle the paperwork, the legalities, the negotiations and even the local customs determining who pays what fees in the transaction.

In short, don't say, "I would like to sell my house by myself. But I don't have the guts to really pull it off!" You can do it.

Another more valid reason for not selling FSBO is the time and effort involved. Many people lead busy, hectic lives and simply don't have the time or energy to devote to selling their homes by themselves. If you're in this group, you're probably not hard to identify. You're the sort who would rather hire a gardener than mow the lawn, take your car to a mechanic rather than change the oil yourself or call a plumber when you have a leaky faucet rather than buy a washer and fix it.

In short, there are a great many who find it perfectly reasonable to pay a full commission to an agent to do it for them, rather than do the work involved for themselves. If you're in this group, I suggest that you at least read the chapters on taxation, mortgage basics, writing disclaimers, closing and working with agents to get yourself up-to-speed on what's involved in a real estate transaction. This information should help you get the best deal and the best agent.

If you do have the time an energy, on the other hand, by all means do spend it getting a quicker sale and/or making more money by selling FSBO. Everything you need to know to do it successfully you can learn from this book.

Remember, there's no law, no custom, no person standing in your way saying that you can't sell your own home. I've owned dozens of properties. Some I've sold through agents. Others I've sold myself. The real truth that I've found beyond any author of any book trying to get you to go FSBO, or any agent pressuring you for a listing is that most people have the ability to sell their homes by themselves.

A Trial FSBO

Making decisions is hard work. Trying to decide whether to sell your home (for most people, the largest investment of a lifetime) by yourself or through an agent can be doubly hard. Therefore, I have an easy way out—a trial FSBO.

If you're not sure whether or not you'd like to sell by FSBO, give it a trial period. Before you list, give yourself a week, a month, three months (probably the most reasonable time period) or whatever. Set a deadline and until that deadline expires, do everything you possibly can to sell by owner. Then, if you still haven't sold the house, you can always list it and hope an agent will.

The Tools You Need

In this book I'll show you what you need to know to sell by owner. We'll consider price, fix-up, neighborhood, advertising, dealing with legalities, talking to buyers and more. This book contains the tools you need to do a FSBO successfully.

With work, you'll get your house sold before your deadline and you can celebrate. I'm betting that it will sell—profitably and quickly—before then, if you apply what you learn here.

FIGURE 1.1

Checklist To Find Out If You Have the Temperament To Sell FSBO

1. Are you willing to give up evenings and weekends for the next three months?   Yes _____   No _____

2. Will you be willing to let strangers into your home?   Yes _____   No _____

3. Can you be ready to show your home day or night on a moment's notice?   Yes _____   No _____

4. Are you a risk taker?   Yes _____   No _____

5. Are you willing to learn how to do new and different things?   Yes _____   No _____

6. Are you determined to save money on the sale of your home?   Yes _____   No _____

7. Do you want a quick sale?   Yes _____   No _____

8. Are you willing to handle the paperwork yourself?   Yes _____   No _____

9. Are you willing to negotiate face-to-face with a buyer?   Yes _____   No _____

10. Are you a patient person?   Yes _____   No _____

ANSWERS

1. You have to be ready to show the house when the buyers want to see it. Remember, there's no agent to show it for you.

2. You also have to screen the buyers yourself and then let perfect strangers into your house. If you're concerned about security, you're not a good candidate to be a FSBO seller.

FIGURE 1.1 *(Continued)*

3. Spontaneity is needed. A potential buyer who calls wants to see your place *now*. Tell the caller to come back later and you could lose a deal.

4. It's riskier to venture into the unknown and sell FSBO rather than list. But it's also frequently quicker and more profitable.

5. You'll have to work with attorneys, escrow and loan officers, inspectors and others. You'll have to learn about sales agreements and other documents. It's not hard, but it does require determination to succeed.

6.&7. Proper motivation is essential here. If you don't want to save money and sell quickly, why bother going FSBO?

8. You'll need to do some of it.

9. There's no intermediary to blunt the buyer's criticism, anger or frustration. You have to deal with it all and turn it into something positive.

10. You'll need lots of patience to succeed.

SCORE

9 to 10 = Yes. You're a natural FSBO.

7 to 8 = Yes. You need to dwell a little longer on how much money a 5 to 7 percent commission really is.

5 to 6 = Yes. Borderline—try it for a while to see if you like it.

1 to 4 = Yes. Don't waste time. List your house now.

Do You Have the Temperament To Sell by Owner?

Figure 1.1 is a short quiz that may help you decide if you should sell by owner, or run to the nearest agent and list your property.

CHAPTER TWO

Seven Key Steps To Selling a FSBO Successfully

You can sell your house as a FSBO.

However, in order to do it, you will have to take seven steps. If you take these steps, your house will sell. If you don't, chances are that it will languish on the market, causing you nothing but grief and headaches.

The seven steps are not hard, but they are critical. I've put them all in one place so that you can see what they are at a glance and how they fit together (see Figure 2.1).

Let's take the steps one at a time to ensure you understand what they are and what you need to do to get the house sold.

FIGURE 2.1   Seven Steps to a Successful Sale

1. Make up your mind to sell FSBO.
2. Price it right.
3. Get the property ready.
4. Let everyone know it's for sale.
5. Make it available when buyers want to see it.
6. Offer easy-to-buy terms.
7. Don't give up.

1. Make Up Your Mind To Sell FSBO

Selling by owner is simply not as easy as listing. When you list with an agent, that agent should do everything for you, in exchange for a commission. When you sell by yourself, you have to do everything yourself, in exchange for not paying that commission.

To be a successful FSBO seller, you must identify the tasks you need to accomplish and make up your mind to do them. You won't have anyone to prod you. Yes, you can draw on a host of expert advisers including agents, attorneys and escrow and loan officers, but the deal revolves around you. You are the spark plug to make it all happen. If you don't do the work, it won't get done.

In essence, selling FSBO can seem to be a daunting task, at least the first time. Faced with new and unfamiliar things, it's easy to get discouraged. It's easy to say to yourself, "I can't possibly do this!"

The point is that you certainly can. What's needed up front is commitment on your part. If you're determined to do it, you can accomplish it. If you have any doubts, remember that when you successfully sell your FSBO, your efforts will be amply rewarded.

2. Price It Right

In today's market, price is critical. It is *almost* as critical as location. Houses that are priced right will sell. Those that are priced too high will sit there.

The reason, of course, is that during a buyers' market the competition for selling a home is furious. Buyers have plenty of choices, and they invariably select the cheapest houses. If your house isn't priced right, not only will it not sell immediately, it may simply not sell at all.

The biggest mistake you can make is to think, "Because I'm selling FSBO, I can ask more money for my house."

Of course, you probably won't make this critical mistake, but if you know of others who are selling FSBO, remind them that buyers see things differently than sellers. Buyers don't care if it's listed, FSBO or auctioned. They are interested in only one thing after location, and that's price. Give the buyers the right price and they'll buy.

To you, selling FSBO may be significant. It may mean that you're putting in lots of time and effort. And you may be spending big bucks fixing up the house. It's only natural, therefore, that as a FSBO seller you want to recoup the time, money and effort from the buyer. It's not unreasonable to feel that you are entitled to ask more for your house.

The truth, unfortunately, is that entitled or not, you can get only what the house is worth on the market. You can ask anything that you want. You will only get, however, what buyers are willing to pay. Remember, buyers don't care who is selling. They don't care how much sweat and tears or how many dollars you've pumped into the property. As far as they are concerned, that's your problem. Theirs is to get the best possible price.

Thus, the rule for FSBO sellers to remember is that you can't price your property any higher because it's FSBO. In fact, for a quicker sale, you need to price it lower. (Don't make the mistake of pricing it only a few hundred dollars lower thinking that in so doing, you're splitting the commission with the buyer. It doesn't work that way. For the hassle of doing business with a FSBO, buyers already expect a much lower price.)

3. Get the Property Ready

Think of it this way. You can place flour, water, cocoa, eggs, yeast, sugar and food coloring in front of most people, and they'll look at it dispassionately; however, mix it all up, bake it and present them with the finished product and they're most likely to say, "Yum, a chocolate cake!"

Home buyers are no different. Present them with a front yard filled with weeds, unkempt bushes, bare patches of ground, cracked paths, peeling paint, a crummy-looking front door and they're going to say, "Ho-hum."

On the other hand, do the gardening work so that the lawn's mowed and green, the bushes are trimmed, colorful blooming flowers surround a newly painted or brand new wooden door and they'll say, "Now, this is a house worth considering!"

Carry this strategy to the inside of the home with new paint, new wallpaper, cleaned and polished (or new) floors, thinned out furniture and top it off with sweet smells, and those buyers are likely to say, "Yes, I could live here!"

Make the effort. Do the work. It won't cost that much, take that much time or be that hard to do. Getting and keeping your property ready for buyers is essential if you want to sell.

4. Let Everyone Know It's for Sale

Don't keep the fact that you're selling FSBO a secret. Display a good-looking sign prominently in your front yard. Prepare leaflets describing your property, including a picture, and distribute them widely. Make them available on an information box attached to your sign. Put them on bulletin boards in public buildings, the housing offices of corporations and even on display panels in supermarkets.

It pays to advertise. Your ad doesn't have to be big, but it should run regularly and you should change it often (so that buyers don't recognize it as the same property and ignore it).

Find out whether inexpensive advertising is available on local radio and cable TV stations. (There often is.) Try a 30-second commercial there. The right slant can bring you amazing results.

You should talk up your property to all of your acquaintances whether or not they're interested in buying. Someone may know a friend of a friend who's interested, and that person might ultimately become your buyer.

Be friendly with real estate people. Tell them you'll pay them at least a part commission if they find a buyer. (See Chapter 4 for details on how to work out a commission split.) Let agents know that you'll work with them. Agents, after all, are in the business of finding buyers. It would be foolish to ignore them, particularly when you can get them to work for you.

Let agents "cobroke" your property with you for a part commission. Consider open listings, in which you pay any agent or short-term exclusive agency listings, in which you agree to pay only one agent but only for a limited time. Don't sign an exclusive right-to-sell listing unless you plan to take your house off the market as a FSBO and give it entirely to an agent to sell.

5. Make Your Home Available

Making the commitment to sell FSBO means giving up much of your free time. It means that you must be willing to sit at home waiting for buyers who may never show up. If a buyer calls you at eight in the morning on Sunday while you're still sleeping, you'll agree to show the property at nine, even though it means jumping out of bed and working frantically to get the place ready.

Being available for buyers means keeping at least one phone line clear. If you're going to be gone, it means using call forwarding, an answering machine or a family member to catch incoming calls. It means that you're ready to show the house every day of the week *and* that it's clean all of those days.

Don't bother to sell FSBO unless you're willing to do all of the tasks described. If you're half-hearted about it, if you decide to take a two-week vacation three weeks after putting the sign in the front yard, if you tell a buyer who calls that you've got to go to your mother's house for lunch and can't show the property, then don't bother to sell FSBO.

When you list with yourself, you must make the commitments necessary to sell your home successfully. One of the biggest commitments is time. If you can't spend the time, list with an agent who can. A FSBO seller must make the house available. That's just the way it is.

For that period of time until you get the appropriate signatures on the dotted line, you're a slave to buyers. To think anything else is to do yourself a disservice. To attempt to sell FSBO without making yourself and the property always available is simply to be playing at it.

If you truly want to sell FSBO, you'll make the time. If you find that you simply can't make the necessary time, then I strongly suggest you reconsider listing with an agent.

6. Offer Easy-To-Buy Terms

Housing prices today, even after the depressed market of the early '90s, remain high. Cash, on the other hand, is short. Very few people have the cash for the down payment necessary for a purchase.

The easier you can make the purchase for the buyer, the better the chance that your house will sell before your neighbor's house does. There are two big ways that you can help the buyer. The first is with the down payment. The traditional down payment is 20 percent of the sales price. At a sales price of $100,000, that means $20,000 in cash down. In addition, the buyer must pay closing costs, which could easily be another $5,000. Therefore, to purchase your house in the traditional way, a buyer would need $25,000.

Undoubtedly, there are buyers who have $25,000 in their jeans and who are ready to plunk it down on a house. However, I can assure you that for every buyer who has $25,000 to put down, there are five buyers who have only $15,000. Therefore, you can increase the chances of finding a buyer for your house by a factor of five or more simply by reducing the down payment.

If you can offer buyers 10 percent down on the same $100,000 house, they have to come up with only $10,000 plus $5,000 for closing costs. If you do this, you are going to find at least five times as many buyers who will be able to consider purchasing your house.

You can do this by accepting a 10-percent second mortgage on your property. Or, if your house is mostly paid off, you can carry an even bigger second mortgage, making it even easier for the buyer to qualify. If your house is fully paid off, you can even carry a first mortgage.

The point is that when you make it easier for buyers to purchase, you make it easier on yourself to sell.

The same holds true with terms. Just as more buyers have fewer dollars to put down, more buyers also have less income from which to make mortgage payments. If you take back any paper (a mortgage of some sort), consider offering a lower interest rate or at least lower monthly payments. For every buyer who can afford to pay $1,000 a month, there are five buyers who can afford $700 a month.

It's like a pyramid (see Figure 2.2). Those with less money and less income are at the wider bottom. Those with more money and more income are at the pointed top. The more you can appeal to those at the bottom of the pyramid, the bigger the base of potential buyers you can attract.

This is not to say that there aren't problems inherent with lower down payments and easier terms. Chapter 9 details many of them.

7. Don't Give Up

Rome wasn't built in a day. Most seemingly instant successes are the result of repeated attempts after repeated failures. Most of those who succeed aren't any brighter, more industrious or more knowledgeable than you.

In short, you too can sell your house FSBO.

The trouble is, you may not be able to sell it the first day or the first week, or even the first month. Time may become some-

FIGURE 2.2   Pyramid of Buyers

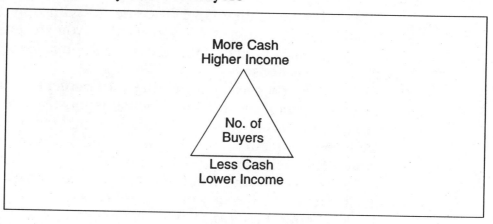

thing you'll learn to hate. You'll stay home on weekends waiting for someone to call or knock on your door. Or, suddenly, three or four people will call and then come by. Or you'll spend so much time cleaning and polishing, painting and trimming that you'll be sick of it. You'll begin to tell yourself you need a vacation from house selling!

In the short term, you may come to hate your house and the process of selling it.

That's okay as long as you don't give up it before your deadline (noted in the last chapter). Remember, for every house there's a buyer. It may just be that yours hasn't come along yet.

Hang in there. Your buyer will show up, if you're sufficiently persistent.

CHAPTER
THREE

A Quick Sale Plan

Once you've decided to sell by owner, you need a plan. In other words, to accomplish your task, it's a good idea to have a recipe, a formula for how to proceed.

In this chapter we will look at the three basic ingredients necessary to help you sell quickly by owner. No, we won't cover all the parts involved, and we won't cover each of these in detail—they're all handled in subsequent chapters. We're simply going to see how to jump-start the process so you can be up and running.

Here are the three basic steps you need to take to get started:

1. Work on your salesmanship.
2. Fix up the property.
3. Set a reasonable price.

Work on Your Salesmanship

First, you need to feel comfortable about selling. You're going to need a crash course in salesmanship. While we'll have a lot more to say about this in Chapter 7, for now let's just talk about the art itself of selling.

Some people feel that a good salesperson can sell ice cubes to Eskimos and sunlamps to Hawaiians. If you're this type of salesperson, you can sell your house on your own by next week without my or anybody else's help.

On the other hand, if you're a normal human being, you may get along fairly well with people, but you don't have any supertalents when it comes to selling. Rest assured, you don't need any.

I have found that when selling real estate, or anything else for that matter, the key is to establish a relationship of trust with the person to whom you're selling. Beyond that, the product should sell itself, assuming it doesn't have a problem.

If you establish a working relationship with the buyer and have a good house that the buyer wants, you merely have to nod in the right places, point out the obvious, reassure the faint of heart and sign on the dotted line. If you have a bad house or the buyer doesn't want it, you're not going to sell it to that prospect now or later, so don't worry about it.

Establish Trust

As the seller of a home dealing directly with a buyer, you are suspect. The buyer suspects that you will do anything and everything to sell that home including lying and cheating. The buyer sees you as the adversary. Therefore, if you're going to deal effectively with that buyer and come to terms that are acceptable in a successful sale, you have to establish trust. How do you do that?

The way to win trust is to be trustworthy. It sounds simple, yet is complicated. Here are the rules:

Never Offend the Buyer

This is far easier to say than to do. Basically you must keep things strictly on business level. If the buyer says that your favorite rose bush looks like a weed, you don't have to agree. But, you don't have to disagree. You can simply point out that roses come in all shapes and sizes.

Ways To Win the Trust of the Buyer

1. Never personally offend the buyer.

2. Never hide a defect in your property.

3. Never lie about anything involving the sale.

4. Never offer to do something you can't do.

If the buyer notes that the color you've painted the stones over your fireplace is hideous, you don't have to get agitated and protest that florid pink goes great over river stones. Simply nod, acknowledging the buyer's opinion, and move on.

The point is simple. As soon as you do anything to offend the buyer, you turn a business deal into a personal disagreement, and *no one* wants to deal with someone he or she doesn't like. Offend the buyer and you could lose a deal.

Never Hide a Defect

Chances are that if you attempt to hide a defect, it will come out sooner or later. For example, you seal and paint some cracks in the walls that are caused by a broken foundation. As soon as the buyer notices the bad foundation and hidden cracks or finds them through an inspection, he or she will distrust you. A buyer who might otherwise be willing to go ahead with the sale if the foundation is fixed, or if there is an adjustment in price, will now wonder what else you've concealed.

A buyer who distrusts you won't want to deal with you and the sale may be lost.

Never Lie about the Property or the Deal

You state that the roof is perfect; it never leaks. But the buyer discovers moisture in the attic. You attempt to cover your tracks by saying it's just condensation or maybe a leaking pipe. Then the buyer notices light coming through between the shingles and concludes that you're a liar, not to be trusted or dealt with. A potential deal could be lost.

Never Say You'll Do Something You Can't Do

You say that you know all about real estate financing, and you'll help the buyer get a loan. You promise that the buyer can qualify for a 90 percent loan, but, after he or she agrees to buy, you both discover that the maximum loan the buyer can get is 80 percent. The buyer can't complete the purchase as negotiated and, feeling cheated, won't come up with more money. The deal may be lost.

The Bottom Line

In short, always be courteous, reasonable and truthful. If you do, the buyer will soon see that you are someone who he or she can work with and who can be counted upon . . . and will want to deal with you. If you don't, you'll find that distrust sours every buyer with whom you deal. Remember, if you try to hide something or lie, little inconsistencies will do you in. Buyers, who are naturally suspicious, are looking for those inconsistencies. Honesty is the key to establishing a relationship with the buyer. The buyer doesn't have to like you (although that does help), but must respect you if the two of you are to conclude a successful real estate sale.

Fix Up the Property

If you want to sell quickly, you must have a better-looking house. We'll devote an entire chapter to the ins and outs of fixing up your property, but for now, let's just say that buyers have no imagination. You can talk until you're hoarse pointing out how much better the house will look with a coat of paint, but, until it's painted, the buyers simply won't see it. Therefore, fix it up.

Paint and basic landscaping are a must. We'll see other things you can do shortly. However, here's the rule:

 Fix Up Everything

- Fix the entrance.

- Paint or replace the front door.

- Paint the outside of the house.

- Paint the inside of the house.

- Remove any furniture that crowds rooms or looks bad.

- Landscape the front yard.

- And do more.

Assuming that you're not trying to rehab your property, a good rule-of-thumb is to do those things that are inexpensive first, then work outward from there. Paint, wallpaper, flowers/shrubs/lawn and getting rid of debris all count. Do these simple things and it will make a world of difference to every potential buyer. (If you are attempting to rehabilitate your house, check into my other book, *The Home Remodeling Organizer,* Chicago: Dearborn Financial Publishing, Inc., 1995.)

Set a Reasonable Price

The hardest thing of all is to be realistic about price. If you price your home low enough, the current market environment makes almost no difference. You will get a sale. Find out the selling price of comparable houses in the recent past and price yours accordingly. (In Chapter 5, we'll see exactly how this is done.)

The trouble is that too many of us are unrealistic. The most chilling phrase I know of in a real estate deal comes when a seller says, "I have a price in my mind." The truth is that it doesn't matter what price you have in mind.

You may think your house is worth what the highest-priced house on your street sold for two years ago. You may feel it's worth the sum total of what you've spent on plants, weed control, carpeting, upgrading and painting. You may feel it's worth what the mortgage appraiser or the county tax assessor told you.

The truth is, it's not worth any of those things. It's worth only what a buyer is willing to pay. If a buyer will pay less than those other figures, you won't sell until you bring your price down to that realistic level. You want to sell? Price your house realistically. You'll sell it right away.

Quick Sale Checklist

In this chapter we've briefly looked at those factors that will help you sell your home quickly. Just in case there's something you don't remember (or don't want to remember), Figure 3.1 is a checklist to help you. The right answers are given at the bottom, as though you'd need to look them up! When you're handling all these items on the checklist correctly, you will have trouble keeping those buyers away from your door!

This checklist is a gentle way of getting at a serious problem: too often, too many of us are unrealistic about defending our property, our salesmanship and our home's appearance and price. In the following chapters we'll delve into each area in detail to see what works and what doesn't. Remember: if your goal is to sell quickly, you can do it.

FIGURE 3.1

☑ **Checklist for a Quick Sale**

SALESMANSHIP

1. Make the buyer your friend?   Yes _____   No _____

2. Forget to mention those bad things about your house that the buyer will never discover?   Yes _____   No _____

3. Exaggerate only occasionally?   Yes _____   No _____

4. Promise the world because the buyer won't remember what you said?   Yes _____   No _____

5. Make the buyer respect you by never lying, hiding or promising what you can't deliver?   Yes _____   No _____

FIX IT UP

6. Do the expensive work first?   Yes _____   No _____

7. Do the cosmetic work first?   Yes _____   No _____

8. Concentrate on bathrooms?   Yes _____   No _____

9. Work on the back yard?   Yes _____   No _____

10. Fix up the front and paint?   Yes _____   No _____

PRICE IT TO SELL

11. Use the highest price ever received in your neighborhood?   Yes _____   No _____

12. Go with the mortgage lender's price?   Yes _____   No _____

13. The tax assessor's price?   Yes _____   No _____

FIGURE 3.1 *(Continued)*

14. The price you really would like to get?   Yes _____   No _____

15. The price a buyer will pay?   Yes _____   No _____

ANSWERS

1. Yes, of course.

2. No. You never know what the buyer will discover.

3. No. Never exaggerate; it shows you lack judgment and have a tendency toward white lies. As far as the buyer is concerned, there are only black lies.

4. No. Buyers, like elephants, never forget.

5. Yes, even though it may be the hardest thing you've ever done when it comes to that old dog of a house you are selling.

6. No. Do the expensive work last; that way the house may sell before you have to do it.

7. Sure. It's the cheapest and will usually make the biggest impression.

8. No. Bathrooms are expensive to fix, although cleaning them so they're spotless won't hurt.

9. No, unless you want to be barbecuing back there for many years to come.

10. You bet. It's what the buyer sees first and first impressions are the most important.

11. No, unless you want to wait for the next big real estate boom to sell.

12. Why, when you can go to a different mortgage lender and get a different appraisal?

13. After seeing what happens to your taxes, would you rely on your tax assessor's judgment?

14. Fantasyland time.

15. Yes, that's the only price that counts. See Chapter 5.

CHAPTER

FOUR

Getting Agents To Work with You

Remember the old expression, "Keep your eye on the dough-nut and not the hole?" It applies when selling FSBO.

Your goal is to sell your home. You want to do it any legiti-mate way that you can, and if an agent can sell it with you, at less than a full commission, you'd be crazy not to go along. Remem-ber, the agent is not the enemy. Your true enemy is time.

If you can save time by working with an agent, it's usually to your advantage to do so. Furthermore, an agent can provide you with many valuable services, not the least of which is helping with the documents and paperwork.

In addition, an agent has resources that are not available to you as a FSBO seller, including many more contacts with potential buyers than you're likely to get. Keep in mind that no matter how much effort you pour into selling your home, you're still a part-time seller. (You're working full-time at your regular employment.) The agent, on the other hand, presumably works full-time at selling. It stands to reason that he or she will see a lot more buyers than you will.

Sharing a Listing

The real question for most sellers often comes down to money. How do you get an agent to work on selling your house if you'd rather not pay a full commission? The answer is sharing a listing with the agent.

For example, consider documents. In Chapter 6 I suggest working with an agent/attorney for a flat fee, arranged in advance, to have that person handle the documents.

Another method is to share the costs and work load. For example, you pay for some of the advertising and promotion as well as help show the property. The agent pays for some costs, does the negotiation and handles the paperwork for a reduced commission. Some agents these days will go along with this arrangement. If you're the sort who wants to sell FSBO, then this type of agent may be for you. One such national franchise is Help-U-Sell. Others are springing up in most communities. We'll have more to say about this shortly.

Listing with Agents

Most people think that to list with an agent, they must pay a full commission. As we've noted, that's not necessarily the case. One of the most common ways of sharing a listing occurs when a broker calls and says something like, "I've seen your FSBO sign and I have a party who I think would like to buy your house. Will you pay a commission if I bring them by and they decide to purchase?"

A wise answer would be, "Certainly, I'll pay you a 'selling commission.'" A "selling commission" is usually half the full commission, (for example, 3 instead of 6 percent). The agent comes by with the prospective buyer and if there's a sale, you pay half a commission.

What have you gained? A very quick sale. What has the agent gained? A quick sale without a lot of presale work invested. It's strictly a "win-win" situation for both of you. More on this is discussed under "open listings."

Sharing the Work Load in Finding a Buyer

We've already broached the subject of a shared listing. As noted, you do some of the work and pay some of the costs in finding a buyer and the agent does some. Does this really work out? It can. Let's consider what you would typically be responsible for and what the agent's duties would be (see Figure 4.1. Note: The breakdown of duties between seller and agent will vary with different agents, so check around).

From the list shown in Figure 4.1, it should be obvious what is meant by a "shared listing." (Note: Shared listing is a descriptive term, not a technical term—agents will suggest using different kinds of specific listings, which we'll discuss shortly.)

Let's go over it carefully to be sure we understand the finer points. In a traditional listing, you don't do anything except get your house in shape and get out of the way. The agent takes care of everything else, in return for a full commission.

In a shared listing, you pay for part of the advertising (and, thus, have a voice in how often, where and how big the ads run), you show the property yourself (the agent may call and say that someone is coming out and it's up to you to handle the potential buyers) and you may need to turn that prospect into an actual buyer using some sales techniques.

Usually you won't have to worry about the paperwork, and the technical negotiations will, presumably, all be handled by the agent. In other words, in a shared listing, you do almost as much work as if you were selling your property as a straight FSBO. So what's the advantage in sharing a listing in order to find a buyer?

FIGURE 4.1

 Shared Listing

Your responsibilities:

- Fix up/clean up the property.

- Pay for part of the advertising.

- Show the property.

- Handle some of the negotiations with the buyer.

Agent's responsibilities:

- Put a sign on your property.

- Pay for part of the advertising.

- Find buyers.

- Handle the paperwork.

The Advantages of a Shared Listing

The biggest advantage is exposure.

With a shared listing, the agent can, presumably, spread the word about your home to a network of other agents. Typically, your house also will be put onto a multiple listing service so that virtually all of the agents in the area can work on it. This increases your exposure enormously and now you potentially get the services of all those other agents. While your agent may simply send someone over to look at the property, a cobroker agent (one who is cooperating with yours) will typically escort potential buyers through.

Finally, the commission structure is lower. In some cases, you pay a flat fee up front, perhaps as low as 1 percent of the asking price, and then pay an additional amount, say another couple of percent, later on if the agent produces a buyer. If no buyer is found, your up-front fee is all you pay.

Regardless, the cost to you is usually less than what you would pay through a traditional agent relationship. In a way, it's as though you were selling both through an agent and as a FSBO. Ideally, you would get the benefits of both worlds.

The Disadvantages of a Shared Listing

On the other hand, it isn't all peaches and cream. Since the commission structure for a shared listing is lower than that for a traditional listing, other agents may be less enthusiastic about co-broking (working with) your lister. Some agents may steer their prospects away from your property. (They're not supposed to do that, but in the real world things don't always work out the way they are supposed to.)

Furthermore, in a traditional listing, the listing agent may be inclined to work harder to sell your property. In a shared arrangement, particularly if you've paid an up-front fee, the agent may simply put a sign on your property, list it on the network and then sit back and wait.

Finally, if someone sees the sign on your property and calls the agent, the agent may in turn just call you and tell you to show this prospect your property. If this person later buys, you will undoubtedly be required to pay an additional amount. From one perspective, if the sign on the property had your phone number, you might have gotten the sale entirely by yourself and saved the entire commission.

Listing Agreements

Agents use a variety of listing agreements. We'll talk about three of them here: exclusive right-to-sell, exclusive agency and open agency.

1. Exclusive Right-To-Sell

With this type of listing, you owe the agent a commission regardless of who sells the property, even if you sell the property entirely by yourself. This agreement usually extends to people who were shown the property even if they buy for a set time after the listing expires (often 90 days).

It's the usual agreement in a traditional listing. The idea behind it is that if the agent is paying for advertising and devoting time and effort to the sale of your property, he or she has to be assured that you won't undercut him or her by selling directly to a prospect.

2. Exclusive Agency

Here, the agreement is that if any agent brings in a buyer, whether it's the agent with whom you listed or any other, you have to pay a commission to your agent. However, if you find a buyer entirely on your own (meaning that buyer never contacts any agent), you don't owe the commission to anyone. The idea here is that your agent is protected from other agents coming in and dealing directly with you, but is not protected if you find a buyer by yourself.

This is the type of agreement sometimes used with a shared listing when you pay an up-front fee. In other words, you may pay the agent $1,000 up front whether the house sells or not. For this, the agent agrees to put the house on the multiple listing exchange, put up a sign and handle all the paperwork.

If any agent finds a buyer, you will then pay an additional fee. If you find a buyer, you're out only the original grand.

3. Open Agency

Here, you tell any and all agents who come by that you will give them a commission if they find a buyer. If they don't find a buyer, then there's no commission to pay. This arrangement has specific advantages and certain times when it can be used.

An "open listing" is basically a nonexclusive listing. Many agents won't consider it, feeling that they might end up spending a lot of time selling a property, only to have it sold out from under them either by you or by another agent. (Note: In this listing you pay a commission only to the agent who brings in a seller. The agents are not required to split the commission among themselves, although they may.) The real question, however, is why would you want to give an open listing?

Let's now look at it in detail. You've got your house up FSBO. You've invested in a sign, leaflets, information box, advertising and so forth, and there you sit waiting for a buyer to come in.

Then, one day, a real estate agent drives up and says that she has a client who might be interested in your home. This person has been looking for a home like yours in your price range and she would like to bring him by. However, she certainly won't bring the client over unless you're willing to pay a commission.

Since your goal is to sell your property, you tell her to go ahead, and she has you sign an open listing agreement. Basically, this says that if you sell to her buyer, you will pay her a commission. On the other hand, if you sell to someone you find or to someone brought in by another agent, you don't have to pay her anything at all.

You want to sell. Here's a potential buyer. Why not? As noted earlier, if you're smart, you'll give this agent her open listing. After all, her client might actually fall in love with the property and purchase it from you. (Note: To avoid conflicts over who initially brought whom to see the property, it is vital that you keep a list of prospective buyers. More on this is in Chapter 9 on showing your home.)

By the way, with this type of listing you can't cut the agent out by calling her buyer later on suggesting that the two of you get together without the agent. A properly drawn open listing agreement is binding on the buyer for a considerable time after the property is shown.

Commission Splitting on an Open Listing

How much of a commission should you pay in an open listing arrangement? If the agent brings in a buyer, should you pay a full commission of 5 to 7 percent (depending on your area of the country)?

I wouldn't. Keep in mind that agents rarely get the entire commission on any sale themselves. Almost every sale involves a split. While there's no hard-and-fast rule, two common splits are 50 percent to the selling office and 50 percent to the listing office, and 40 percent to the listing office and 60 percent to the selling office ($^{50}/_{50}$ and $^{40}/_{60}$).

If an agent has a client and asks if you would give him or her an open listing, why not say, sure, and I'll split the commission with you the same way as is commonly done in this area. If the going rate happens to be 5 percent and it's a $^{50}/_{50}$ split, that means that you'll give the agent 2 1/2 percent, if the client pans out and makes the deal.

Possible Abuses

Real estate agents all know that every FSBO is a potential listing. Although it is unethical for them to do and the vast majority will not, an unscrupulous agent may call pretending they have a buyer (when they don't) and solicit an open listing from you. They may then trot someone through your property who could be their brother-in-law or a friend. (How do you know who the client is?)

The point of this little charade is to get close to you. Once you've given an agent an open listing, for example, and that agent has brought a client by, even if the client does not purchase your home, you might be more inclined to deal with the agent. In short, the ploy could result in the agent's getting a more traditional listing from you sometime later on down the road.

One way to handle this is to offer to split the commission with the agent on a one–day open listing. In other words, the listing is only for the one time the agent shows the property to this very interested client. This says in a most dramatic way that you're not interested in playing games. If the agent does indeed have a legitimate client, he or she should be willing to cooperate with you for half the commission on this one buyer and no other. After all, it's the sale that counts.

If the agent is only playing games, a one–day half commission offer will often make it not worth the time to go through the phony client routine.

Dealing with Agents Who Stop By Only To List

Unfortunately, many FSBO sellers are so pestered by agents that as a result, they won't even talk to them, let alone agree to give them an open listing. Some will even hang a small sign on their for-sale sign that says, Principals Only or No Agents.

This is a serious mistake because it hurts you. Remember that your goal is to sell the home. The more people working on that goal, the better. Keeping agents away, in most cases, will only delay the sale of your property.

My suggestion is that you hang a smaller sign on your property that reads, "Will Cooperate with Brokers" (see Figure 4.2). This tells agents two things. The first is that if they have a client, you will give them at the least an open listing presumably for half a commission. (Agents are well aware of this arrangement and if they come by, will probably be ready to accept it.)

Thus, they don't see you as an adversary, but as a possible source of a commission. They will want to work with you.

Second, it puts them on notice that you are serious about handling the sale yourself. "Cooperate" does not mean that you are willing to give them a traditional listing. In the trade, it means that you will split the deal, including the commission, with them. In other words, you will work as an equal with any agent who has a client.

The house, in effect, is your own listing. You'll be willing to cobroke (cooperate with brokers) on it.

FIGURE 4.2   Additional Sign To Show Cooperation with Brokers

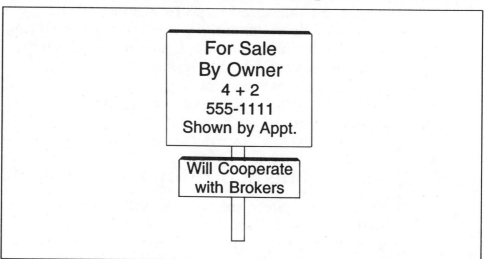

This shows that you know what you're doing and can earn the respect of agents. (A sign that tells agents to stay away, on the other hand, often only serves to earn their disdain.)

Further, such a sign puts agents on notice that they're going to get only half a commission from you, not a traditional listing's full commission. Surprisingly, the above message on your sign, in my experience, results in far fewer agents pestering you and far more serious agents stopping by with clients. It may seem like a contrary thing to do, since your goal is to sell FSBO, but if it works, why not go with it?

Pricing Your Property When You List It with a Professional

Many FSBO sellers use a straightforward approach to price when listing their property either for an open/half commission listing or an exclusive right-to-sell/full commission listing.

They take the price they were asking as a FSBO and then add to it the commission. That becomes their new asking price.

Bad move. It's true that the agent, who is in the business, has more contacts via the multiple listing service, gets more potential buyers to see them and has a better chance, statistically, of locating the right buyer than you do.

It's not true that this input can be added in dollars to your sales price. The value of your home is what a buyer who is ready, willing and able to purchase will pay. It's not a penny more. As many people have dramatically found out, the market value of your property does not depend on what you want to get, how much you owe or whether you sell by owner or through an agent. It's simply what the market will bear at the time you are selling.

Thus, if you add the cost of the commission to the price you were asking as a FSBO, and you had the house priced correctly, you will have just priced yourself out of the market. Potential buyers will simply not bother. They will realize that there are other houses available, as good as yours, for less money, and they will buy those houses instead of yours.

The sad truth is that if you list, in 99 cases out of a 100, you'll end up paying the commission out of your equity, that is, out of your pocket. You won't be able to add that commission to the price and still get a sale. What you gain is the sale itself. Of course, avoiding the commission was one of the main reasons that you decided to sell FSBO in the first place, wasn't it?

Another problem comes with adding to the price on open listing commissions. If you're asking, for example, $100,000 for your home and you give an open listing to an agent, only at a price of $103,000 (adding in the commission amount), you've potentially put yourself in a real bind and you could lose the deal.

At some point the buyer will likely find out that you were only asking $100,000 FSBO and will not want to pay a penny more for going through an agent, but that buyer was brought in by the agent and your listing agreement precludes you from selling to him or her unless you go through that agent.

So, unless you're in a fast-rising real estate market in which the buyer may be willing to pay a premium, you may end up compromising by reducing the price. You still may end up getting less. What's worse, that buyer may get worried about your reliability and credibility. He or she may decide that it's simply too risky to deal with you and, instead, buy someone else's home.

In short, by trying to have two prices at the same time, one a FSBO price and the other a listed price, you could be cutting your own throat when finding buyers.

The Danger of Listing Too High

Regardless of what I've just said about pricing and commissions, the tendency remains for FSBO sellers to want to add the commission onto the price when they list. It's just human nature.

In the past the worst this could do would be to slow down the sale. Many agents would take a house listed too high in the hope of convincing the seller to later reduce the price. The theory was that any listing, even one too high in price, was better than no listing. However, when the market is not strong, as has been the case during the recent real estate recession, homes that are priced too high sometimes don't sell, even after the price has been reduced!

I have seen this happen dozens of times. The FSBO seller adds on the commission and lists the house perhaps 5, 6 or 7 percent above market, but the market is very tight with a great many houses for sale. Thus, buyers can afford to be choosy and they ignore the overpriced property.

Time goes by a month, two, three. Eventually the seller realizes the mistake and lowers the price to where it should have been to begin with, but by now, the house is a stale item. It's been listed for so long that agents figure there's something wrong with it and don't bring buyers in. Even at a fair price, the house doesn't get the attention it deserves, and, hence, it doesn't sell. Often the poor seller must reduce the price to below market in order to attract attention and get a sale.

The days when you could list too high and always come down are long gone. In truth, today the best chance you may have of selling is in the first month of a listing. So you'd better have the house priced correctly, right away.

When Should You List with an Exclusive Agent?

At the very beginning of this book, I suggested that you should set a time limit on selling your home FSBO. This time limit can be the most important thing you do with regard to selling.

Remember, the length of the time limit isn't important. It can be a week, a couple of months or even a year. What's important is that after a set period of time has elapsed, you will *stop trying to sell the property entirely by yourself* and will seek the aid of an agent paying a full commission under an exclusive-right-to-sell listing.

I think it's worth a few sentences to reiterate why this is important. Once again: it's a matter of keeping your eye on the doughnut and not the hole. The goal is to sell your property. While you may have secondary goals of saving money or learning about transactions, none of that will matter if your home never sells.

If you do everything right as a FSBO seller, you should be able to sell by yourself. But maybe your house just doesn't sell. Why it doesn't sell may not matter. Maybe there's something you're not doing right—the house isn't fixed up well enough, you aren't offering the right financing, your price is too high, the market's terrible, you've got a very undesirable location. There are any number of possible reasons.

The point is, the house hasn't sold. You set the time limit when you started your FSBO; now it's time to consult with a professional, an agent. After you've given it a fair shot on your own, you'd be doing yourself a disservice not to try a different avenue. Not listing when you've honestly tried to sell your home is like ignoring reality and putting your head ostrichlike in the sand. Bite the bullet and accept an exclusive-right-to-sell listing to a committed agent.

Remember, your goal—selling your home.

CHAPTER

FIVE

Price It Right and It Will Sell

Nothing is more important when selling a home than setting the right price. It's the single most important decision you have to make when you sell FSBO (after making the FSBO decision itself).

If your price is too high, buyers will simply not bother to make offers. If it is too low, you'll lose money. What you need to find is just the right price—one that attracts buyers yet gets you the highest possible amount of money.

Warning: It's important to remember that most FSBOs are put on the market at a higher price than competing houses that are listed with agents. That's what keeps them from selling.

The Lame Seller

One would logically think that real estate agents would be afraid of FSBOs. After all, they represent competition. The opposite is actually true. Most agents love to see FSBOs for two reasons. The first we've already mentioned: FSBOs are typically priced higher than competing homes. Hence, wise agents will sometimes encourage buyers to stop by FSBOs for comparison. Some agents will even accompany their clients to FSBOs so that the prospective buyers can see for themselves, by comparison, just how good the listed deals are that the agent is offering.

The other reason is that FSBOs are an excellent source of listings. Agents know that a FSBO priced much higher than comparable homes in the area won't sell. Eventually the seller is going to get tired of showing the property and waiting endlessly for a buyer who never appears and list.

Price Is Everything (Almost)

Remember, the big reason that most FSBOs don't sell is the price. (A good lesson here is to go into the corner of the room and repeat to yourself three times, Price, Price, Price!) If you want to sell, particularly in today's market, you have to have a realistic price.

Why do most FSBO sellers set their prices too high to attract prospective buyers? The seller is often focusing on the wrong goal. What you, the seller, should be interested in most is selling your property. What often happens, however, is that a homeowner who decides to sell without an agent begins focusing on two different things: how much he or she wants for the property and how much he or she can save by not paying an agent's commission; hence, more money in the bank. The seller ends up with unrealistic expectations of getting a fabulous sale and saving money in the process. The real end result is a house that's priced too high. It's higher than comparable houses are selling for and it keeps buyers from making offers.

You Must Sell Lower Than the Market

Here's a second pointer to remember. For most buyers, a FSBO is a less desirable home on which to make an offer than a listed property. This may seem to fly in the face of arguments that have long been given saying that buyers prefer FSBOs.

It's quite true, for example, that when you place your ad in the newspaper, the most compelling words you can write are, "By Owner." That's almost guaranteed to catch buyers' interest.

What's never mentioned, however, is *why* buyers are drawn to FSBOs. The reason, quite simply, is that they are looking for a bargain. They know that agents are unlikely to show them your house; hence, they want to check it out to be sure that they're not missing anything. They also realize that you're not paying a commission to an agent, and anticipate that you'll pass on the savings to them.

When they call or stop by, however, and discover that your house isn't any cheaper and, in fact, may be more expensive than others they have looked at, they will almost always drop you like a hot potato. Buyers don't really want to argue with you. If it doesn't cost any more, they'd rather have the insulation of dealing with an agent rather than an owner.

Furthermore, the minute they walk into your house and realize you're not offering it for less, they'll assume that the real reason you listed is to save for yourselves the commission an agent would charge, not for them. In addition, if you're asking more than the market price, buyers will believe the real reason is that you refuse to accept what the market will bear for your home.

Either way, you'll be branded as an unmotivated and difficult seller. In short, buyers won't want to deal with you. Why should they, when they can deal far more easily through an agent on a lower-priced, listed home?

Why Buyers Actually Prefer Agents

Although we've touched on it, let's stop for a moment to consider this: The real reason most buyers feel uncomfortable dealing directly with the seller is confrontation. Buyers may hate the way you've arranged the backyard, but they don't want to tell you because they're afraid they'll offend you. They won't, however, hesitate to tell an agent who is representing the owner.

They might love the floor plan and the way your kitchen has been updated, but they won't tell you for fear you'll stick to your price even more. They will tell an agent when making an offer.

They might really like your house, but they want to offer you much less than you're asking. However, they might find it hard to come right out and make that kind of offer, fearing that you'll be insulted. In short, most buyers dislike even the suggestion of a confrontation with a seller. That's why they prefer to talk to an agent.

How To Overcome Buyer's Resistance to a FSBO

Basically, when you sell FSBO, you're at a disadvantage. Given two identical houses located side by side, both offered at the same price, but one a FSBO and the other listed with an agent, the listed house will sell first every time.

 Rule for Pricing

If you sell FSBO, you're presumably saving on the commission and have some room to play with. So give the buyers the price discount that they want, and you will sell your house faster and probably net more money.

The question becomes, how do you overcome the disadvantage? The quickest answer is offering a lower price. The mistake that most of those who sell FSBO make is thinking that they can keep the whole commission savings for themselves. You can't do that and realistically expect to sell the property in short order.

The Right Way To Price Your FSBO

It all comes back to goals. Is your goal to save money? Or, is it to sell your property? If it's to sell your property, you have an excellent chance of succeeding as a FSBO, because you're in a position to offer it for less.

Let's consider the following example. You've investigated the area (as explained later in this chapter) and find that homes just like yours are usually listed for around $200,000. You also discover that three properties have sold in the past six months for an average price of $190,000. That means that buyers are typically purchasing for 5 percent less than the listed price.

You also discover that the average commission charged in your area is 6 percent. (As noted, the amount of commission charged by an agent is always negotiable most—run from 5 to 7 percent.) On a $190,000 sale, that amounts to $11,400. Those sellers who sold for $190,000 actually netted out $178,600.

Now, how much do you ask for your house?

Most FSBO sellers would ask at least $200,000. Many would ask a higher amount, figuring that their house, with its unique qualities (every house has unique qualities) is worth more. They hope to save the difference between what the other sellers netted and their own asking price.

$200,000	Price
178,600	Other sellers' net
21,400	Savings

The problem, of course, is that you'll never sell that property at $200,000. You won't even get offers. Buyers will choose to make offers on listed properties at that price (for the reasons we discussed), but not on your FSBO.

But, what if you price your property at, say, $185,000? That's $15,000 less than the price of listed houses. Will you get offers? You bet you will. Buyers who might otherwise pass because of the inconvenience of dealing directly with a seller, all else being equal, will stand in line to deal directly with you if they can save $15,000. Of course, if you sold at $185,000, you would still net $6,400 more than comparable sellers who had listed and sold at

$190,000 and paid a commission. Even if you had to accept a lower offer, say $178,600, exactly what other sellers had netted after a commission, you'd still be far ahead.

Why? Because your house would sell more quickly, and time is not only money, it's also peace of mind.

Keeping Sight of the Goal

You must be absolutely clear on your goal. Are you interested in selling that house as quickly as possible so that you can get on with your life? Or, are you interested only in saving money on the costs of the sale? If you are interested in a quick sale, you have the perfect opportunity with a FSBO because you can offer to sell for so much less than you can by going through an agent.

However, you may be interested in doing both, selling quickly and saving money. Again you're in a great position to do this, because you can still discount your house for, say, as much as you'd pay for half a commission and still make it attractive to buyers. It might take a bit longer to sell than it would with a deep discount, but the result could still be a successful sale.

Finding Out What Your House Is Really Worth

Now that we have the strategy in mind, let's see if we can put it into practice. Let's turn to the process of discovering just what the market for your home is.

Most of us loosely track housing values in our neighborhood. Any time a nearby house sells, we usually try to learn the sales price. After all, that lets us know what our house might be worth.

However, for many of us this process is selective. When we learn that a nearby house has sold for more, we add to the value of our house. However, when prices decline and a nearby house sells for less, we tend to dismiss that lesse sale a market aberration. In other words, most of us add value when the market goes up but don't subtract value when the market goes down. Therein lies a trap that could keep you from selling your home.

Understanding the Market

The truth is that the market doesn't care how much you paid for your home; how much money, how many tears and how much sweat you put into your home; how much you owe on your mortgage; or even how much your home was worth three years ago. All that the market cares about is what a buyer is ready, willing and able to pay *right now.*

That statement can be very sobering, whether you sell with or without an agent. What it means is that your ability to sell in today's market is often linked directly to your ability to forget what you think your house is worth and instead, sell for what a buyer will actually pay.

Perceived Value versus Real Value

The problem is that we all tend to spend money before we get it. A good friend of mine, Chuck, recently sold his house in a terrible housing market. Chuck had bought his home 15 years ago for around $40,000. He had seen it soar in value to over $400,000 back in 1989 at the top of the market. He remembered that figure, $400,000. If he sold for that amount he would have enough money to buy a condominium unit for his wife and himself, pay for his kids' college education and get the gorgeous 30-foot sailboat he had always dreamed about. The problem was that he wanted to sell in 1994, not back in 1989.

When he checked around (we'll see how to appraise your own house shortly), he found that houses just like his were on the market for $325,000 and lower. (They had gone as low as $275,000, but the market had bounced back from there.) The last sale had actually been for $300,000.

It almost drove him to tears. It was obvious he wasn't going to get $400,000 for his house, at least not soon. So much for that dream boat. He put his house up for sale at $375,000. At least there was the condo and the kids' education. When it didn't sell, he lowered the price to $350,000 and then to $325,000. The kids would have to go to much less expensive schools. Chuck was lucky. He finally lowered his price to $300,000 and found a buyer. However, it took him almost a year to get that low. In short, he wasted a year of keeping his house neat and clean, of showing it to lookers and of emotional ups and downs with maybe buyers. In the end, he had to sell for the market price.

If you ask him today, he'll tell you he wishes he had sold for that price right off the bat. "The worst thing was that I wasted a year of my life trying to sell that darn house. It wasn't until it was finally sold that I realized how much of an emotional drain it had been."

Therein lies a great truth of selling: It's better to bite the bullet and sell for a fair price, even if it's much lower than the price you want, just so you can get on with your life. You don't want to make a career of selling your home.

How Long Will It Take To Sell?

Another factor in determining price is time. The sooner you want to sell, the less you should ask. The more you are willing or able to wait, the higher the price you can ask.

A broker friend of mine describes an experiment she did at a meeting of real estate brokers to help determine a home's value. At this meeting, the brokers each stood up and touted one of their homes to the others, hoping that by doing so, they might discover another broker who had a buyer. When my friend stood up, she described a home that was listed for $250,000. When she was done, she asked the assembled brokers, over a hundred of them, "Does anyone have a buyer for this house at $250,000?" When no one replied, she asked, "Does anyone have a buyer at $225,000?" Again there were no responses. "What about at $200,000?" A few brokers raised their hands, tentatively indicating they might have clients who could be interested.

At $175,000 would any of you yourselves be interested in the house? A lot of hands went up. The brokers themselves were interested in buying at that price.

Investment Value

What this story illustrates is how price functions when a house is considered as an investment. Keep lowering the price and you will eventually find a buyer. I call this determining the commodity or the investment value. What it really shows is how important price is to selling.

Shelter Value

What the above example does not take into account is time. At the meeting my friend described, she was just testing to see how much she could get for that house if it were sold then and there. If the price got low enough, there were lots of takers, homebuyers as well as brokers, who would buy figuring they could resell at a profit.

You'll always get plenty of buyers at fire sales or going-out-of-business sales, but prices have to be very low to attract them. On the other hand, if my friend had been willing to wait, she probably could have gotten buyers at a higher price.

If you're willing to wait, you will eventually attract buyers who want to live in the property, not buy it for investment and a quick resale. You hope that these shelter buyers will show up, fall in love with your house and pay more for it than an investor would. This is what I call the shelter value.

The shelter value is what a house will bring when it is for sale for a reasonable length of time, say 90 to 120 days. The shelter value is usually the highest amount you can get for your home. (That's why when you're selling by FSBO you want to cater to buyers who plan to live in the property as opposed to investors who are looking to resell for a profit.) When it comes time to price your home, therefore, you'll undoubtedly want to get the highest shelter value. However, to do so takes time, and you'll have to determine how long you're willing to wait.

Remember that shelter value does not necessarily mean that you can get what you may feel your house is worth or what you have put into it. Shelter value is the highest price that you are likely to get by putting the house up for sale and then waiting for someone who wants to buy the property and live in it.

 Time
_____

You can usually get a higher price if you're willing to wait 90 to 120 days to sell your home. If you want to sell it immediately, you'll usually have to lower the price so it sells more for investment than for shelter value.

How Much To Ask for Your House

Having noted the many pitfalls in determining price, let's now see just how much you can reasonably ask for your house. The charts in this chapter are designed to help you make comparisons with other similar homes that are for sale as well as with those that have recently sold. By finding similar homes for sale and sold, you'll come as close to knowing the true market value of your own home as anyone can, including brokers and appraisers.

The Comparison Method

There are many methods of determining the value of a property. Appraisers use the cost approach, which bases price on cost of reproduction. Investment property is valued by the return on capital it makes. Yet in the final analysis, most properties are valued on the basis of comparison. Find out how much a comparable property sold for and that's the most likely value of yours. This is the method the mortgage appraisers, agents and others involved in real estate use most often to determine the true value of a home. I suggest you use it, too.

The comparison method is really quite simple, in theory. All you do is find four or five houses just like yours in your neighborhood that sold over the past six months, determine the sales price, average it out and that's what your house is worth.

In practice, however, the procedure is quite a bit more complicated. The central problem is that usually it's hard to find good comparables. There may be few sales in your area. Your house may be unique or there may be few models like it. Sales prices themselves may be skewed by seller financing, cash-down sales or other considerations.

You could spend half your life trying to get the perfect comparables—or you could do it the easy way: check with a local agent. Say that you're going to sell FSBO now, but if the property doesn't sell you may list it with the agent. Most agents will be happy to help you. Ask for comparables. Using the computer system available to most offices, they can quickly punch up a list of comparable sales in your area.

You want to be sure the comparables have at least the similarities in Figure 5.1. If you can't find good comparables, then you'll have to do some fancy adjustments. If you find a house that's bigger or fancier than yours and that sold for more, you'll have to guess how much less your house is worth. If you find a tiny, mousy house, much smaller than yours, you'll have to guess how much more yours is worth.

In the end, add up all your comparables and average them out. Be sure to separate the price asked from the price sold. Sold prices, not asking prices, are the true value. Also, try not to use sales more than six months old. Those older than six months may not reflect current market conditions. Voilá! If you've done it correctly, you now should have a good idea of what your home is worth.

To help you, here are a couple of comparable estimating sheets (see Figures 5.2 and 5.3). You may want to duplicate them if you need more. When you get all of your comparables, you'll want to compare them.

Figure 5.4 is a master sheet on which to make your final calculations. To use the Master Comparable Evaluation Sheet, enter the sales price of comparable properties. Then, using the Comparable Estimating Sheet, add an amount for homes that are worse than yours and subtract an amount for homes that are better than

FIGURE 5.1

 Similarities To Look For in Comparables

- Same area of town and similar age

- Same number of bedrooms and baths

- Roughly same square footage

- About same style and design (Don't mix Victorian with Ranch.)

- Roughly same amenities (Don't compare pool homes with those that don't have pools. If you have a fireplace, compare it with another home that also has a fireplace.)

yours. Average the figures and you'll have an average sales price and an average comparable price. If you've done your work scrupulously, the average comparable price should be very close to the market value of your home. Note: You may always want to know the average listing price. When you compare this to the sales price, you'll know how much of a discount buyers are currently getting.

FIGURE 5.2

✓ Comparable Estimating Sheet (1)

Address _____

Square footage _____

Style _____

Condition _____

Bedrooms	Number _____
Baths?	Number _____
Family room?	Yes _____ No _____
Garage?	Yes _____ No _____
2 car	Yes _____ No _____
3 car	Yes _____ No _____
Pool?	Yes _____ No _____
Spa?	Yes _____ No _____
Fireplace?	Yes _____ No _____
Hardwood floors?	Yes _____ No _____
Air-conditioning?	Yes _____ No _____
Good front yard?	Yes _____ No _____
Heavily traveled street?	Yes _____ No _____
General	
Same neighborhood?	Yes _____ No _____
Same style?	Yes _____ No _____
Same size?	Yes _____ No _____
Same amenities?	Yes _____ No _____

List Price $ _____

Sales Price $ _____

FIGURE 5.3

✓ **Comparable Estimating Sheet (2)**

Address _____

Square footage _____

Style _____

Condition _____

Bedrooms	Number _____	
Baths?	Number _____	
Family room?	Yes _____	No _____
Garage?	Yes _____	No _____
2 car	Yes _____	No _____
3 car	Yes _____	No _____
Pool?	Yes _____	No _____
Spa?	Yes _____	No _____
Fireplace?	Yes _____	No _____
Hardwood floors?	Yes _____	No _____
Air-conditioning?	Yes _____	No _____
Good front yard?	Yes _____	No _____
Heavily traveled street?	Yes _____	No _____
General		
Same neighborhood?	Yes _____	No _____
Same style?	Yes _____	No _____
Same size?	Yes _____	No _____
Same amenities?	Yes _____	No _____

List Price $ _____

Sales Price $ _____

FIGURE 5.4

 Master Comparable Evaluation Sheet

	Sale Price	Add/Subtract	Comp Price
House #1	$ _____	$ _____	$ _____
House #2	$ _____	$ _____	$ _____
House #3	$ _____	$ _____	$ _____
House #4	$ _____	$ _____	$ _____
House #5	$ _____	$ _____	$ _____
House #6	$ _____	$ _____	$ _____
House #7	$ _____	$ _____	$ _____

Average Sales Price $ _____

Average Comp Price $ _____

CHAPTER SIX

Understanding Documents

If there's one part of a real estate sale that puts fear in the hearts of the average person considering going FSBO, it's the document. "How will I write up the sales agreement? What of the other documents, some of which I don't even know about? How can I handle these?"

Rest assured, it can be done and with minimum of effort, expense and stress. In this chapter we will see how.

Fear of Paper

Many would-be FSBO sellers ask themselves questions such as, "If I do find a buyer, how do I get him or her to sign up? What document do I use? Do I accept a check as a deposit and, if so, should I give a receipt? What should that receipt say?" In essence, not knowing how to handle the technicalities of a real estate transaction may be keeping you from making the deal yourself and saving oodles of money.

Are these fears justified? Is there something arcane about filling out the sales agreement, deposit receipt and other paperwork? Or, can anyone, including you, do it?

The honest answer is that it is both simple and complex. Yes, you can do it yourself, but you'd probably be wise leaving it to an expert. The legalities behind the paperwork can get you into trouble if you don't know what you're doing. Perhaps a bit of background will help.

The Sales Agreement/Deposit Receipt— Backbone of a Sale

The paper that documents a sale in real estate is called, naturally enough, the *sales agreement.* It should include all the terms and conditions of the sale.

To understand how a sales agreement is put together today, however, a short jaunt into the past is helpful. When I started in real estate over 30 years ago in California, we didn't use a sales agreement. Instead, we used a *deposit receipt.* The deposit receipt, in fact, is still used in many areas.

A deposit receipt is just what it says it is. It's a receipt for a deposit on a piece of property that the buyer gives to the agent or the seller. (Until the buyer puts up some earnest money or a deposit, you really don't have a solid deal.) As part of the receipt, however, all the terms and conditions of the sale were specified. Hence, it became, in effect, a sales agreement.

Way back then, the deposit receipt used to be one legal page long. At the top it contained space to fill in such obvious information as the correct address of the property, the name of the buyer and the amount of the offer (purchase price).

Then a paragraph of legalese specified that the buyer was going to purchase the property according to the terms following, that "time was of the essence" (meaning the deal had to close by a certain date) and a few other conditions. About two-thirds of the remaining page consisted of blank lines. Someone, the seller, the buyer or the agent filled in all the terms.

Finally, there were places for all parties to sign and date the document at the bottom.

Keep in mind that the legal language on this simple document was only a few paragraphs. The agent, the seller or the buyer filled in everything else by hand.

This old deposit receipt form served its function well. It was used to facilitate the sale of millions of pieces of property for decades. However, it had a serious flaw—in many cases it wasn't legally binding.

A seller or a buyer who wanted to get out of the transaction for any reason without penalty frequently could go to court and demonstrate that the document didn't really represent what was intended. Either party could say that the agreement's language was vague or inaccurate or misrepresented their intentions.

Because the deposit receipt was mostly handwritten by agents, sellers or buyers, not by lawyers familiar with creating legally binding language, these contentions were often correct. In other words, the deposit receipt often was fatally flawed. It was rarely the legally binding document intended.

This placed a burden on agents. When either a buyer or a seller got out of a deal because of a flawed deposit receipt written by an agent, the party who felt injured often sued the agent. As a result, such lawsuits increased in the 1970s and agents became gun-shy. When coupled with the skyrocketing price of real estate at the end of the 1970s, the litigation began to involve serious money.

Band-Aids

To correct the situation, agents had their attorneys create *sales agreements* where more of the language was formally printed. Many of the paragraphs that the agents used to write in were now created by lawyers and included as part of the agreement. Instead of a single page of mostly blank lines, these new sales agreements were often two pages long with mostly printed text and only a few paragraphs where the agents would write in the terms of the sale.

The problem, of course, was that any time the agent, or the seller or buyer, wrote in anything at all, there was a chance it wouldn't be legally binding because of incorrect language used. By the late 1980s litigation had demonstrated that even these new contracts with a minimum of language inserted by the agent, buyer or seller could prove to be a minefield. An innocuous sentence inserted by a seller at the time the sales agreement was signed could provide a way out for a buyer later on. The seller might tie up the house for months only to discover that the buyer could walk away from the deal and be entitled to a full return of the deposit! Or, worse, even after the sale was consummated, the seller had moved out and the buyer moved in, inexact language in the contract and an angry buyer might result in litigation in which the seller was forced to pay damages to the buyer.

Today's Sales Agreement

This brings us to the present. Today the consensus seems to be that if it isn't written in by a lawyer, it isn't accurate or binding. Hence, we have the extraordinary situation in which agents are using sales agreements that are often seven, eight, ten or more pages in length. The entire document is a preprinted form and paragraphs for various contingencies are listed. All that the agent, buyer or seller need do is write in the correct names of the parties involved and the property description, check and initial the appropriate paragraphs and fill in the sales price and loan amount. No other writing on the document is recommended.

Furthermore, while state real estate groups usually prepare these forms for their agents/members to use, large real estate franchise companies such as Coldwell-Banker or Century 21 have their attorneys prepare their own forms. Thus, there may be dozens of different formally prepared sales agreements that are used for real estate transactions, even within a given city.

The Plight of the FSBO

Needless to say this puts a FSBO seller at a disadvantage. You don't have your property listed and, as a consequence, you don't have an agent's sales agreement. Yet, to lock up a buyer, you do need a sales agreement that records a receipt for a deposit and spells out the terms of the sale. What do you do?

One answer used by some FSBO sellers, unwisely in my opinion, is to finesse the whole problem by simply going to their local stationery store and purchasing a form called something like, *Sales Agreement for Real Property.* A variety of these are put out by several publishing companies and they contain all of the basics, although in truth, they tend to contain more blank space than legal language.

Other FSBO sellers may have a friend who is an agent, from whom they ask to borrow a couple of sales agreement forms. Since most agents are eager to cooperate with FSBOs in any way, hoping that if the property doesn't sell they will eventually get a listing, they cooperate and hand over some of the forms. (Most agents, however, will first scrupulously cross the name of their company off the form, hoping to avoid any legal entanglements later on.)

Where does this leave the FSBO seller? In a sense it leaves you not much better off than you were before. You have a form to use, but unless you're an attorney or very experienced in selling your own real estate (in which case you probably don't need this kit), you still don't possess the knowledge to fill in the form correctly, even down to knowing which boxes to check and which to leave blank.

The fact remains that if you accept a buyer's deposit, write in the terms of the sale on the document and do the job badly, you could be laying the groundwork for a lot of expensive litigation later on.

The Wrong Way, the Easy Way, the Right Way

This discussion is not intended to frighten you away from handling a FSBO sale because of the paperwork. It's intended only to present a background for some of the problems. There are, however, solutions—good ones.

Here's one that could work well for you. If you are relatively new to selling property on your own, then don't attempt to handle the sales agreement at all. Instead, have someone else who is knowledgeable do it for you. There are two alternatives here.

In many states attorneys who specialize in real estate abound. They make a living by handling the formalities of real estate transactions. Often they prepare the documents necessary to complete a deal.

Why not contact one of these attorneys before you find a buyer and work out an arrangement? The arrangement will go something like this: You will bring in a buyer who has agreed to purchase your home according to certain negotiated terms; the two of you will sit down and the attorney will draw up the sales agreement; the buyer will then examine the document (and perhaps have his or her own attorney examine it); and then you will both sign it.

Simple? Easy? Quick? And it relieves you of the burden of having to worry about correctly filling out a sales agreement, something you probably can't do.

But, what about the cost? Keep in mind that we're talking about an attorney who specializes in real estate transactions. Often these lawyers get as little as $500 for doing the documentary work related to a sale. For just a few dollars more, many should be willing to handle the sales agreement as well.

Just be sure that you make an arrangement with the attorney *before* you need legal services. Your lawyer may be able to give you clues about the information you will supply, so that when you come in, you will have all of it ready.

Dealing with a Nervous Buyer

Another advantage of using an attorney when you're a FSBO seller is dealing with a nervous buyer. One of the problems with selling by FSBO is that buyers tend to be nervous. They tend to be wary of signing anything. Thus, even after you have a buyer who is ready, willing and able to purchase your home, he or she may not want to commit directly to you. After all, the buyer may think, "How am I protected from an unscrupulous seller who wants to cheat me?"

Further, it is a rare buyer who is willing to give a deposit check directly to the seller. As buyers ought to know, once the seller receives that deposit check, it's his money. True, you as a seller might have to pay it back sometime in the future if the deal goes sour. However, until that time, you can stick the money in your account and spend it. If I were a buyer, the last thing in the world I would want to do would be to give my deposit directly to the seller.

However, the real estate attorney provides a reasonable third party for the buyer. A document prepared by you, the seller, may have questionable validity. Buyers are likely to have greater confidence when the agreement is drawn up by an attorney. Furthermore, the buyer can question the attorney and, presumably, get accurate answers.

Also, the buyer can turn the deposit over to the attorney, who may act as an escrow holder, or to an independent escrow company after the deposit receipt is filled out. In short, the attorney becomes a great facilitator for you.

Working with an Agent

In some states, particularly in the West, the use of real estate attorneys is uncommon. Rather, agents handle all of the paperwork in conjunction with title insurance and escrow officers. Finding a real estate attorney in a state such as California, for example, may be akin to the proverbial looking for a needle in a haystack.

However, there's no reason you can't hire an agent to do the paperwork for you. True, agents are there to get a commission by finding a buyer, but they are also there to make money. If you arrange with an agent to handle just the paperwork (that is, filling in the sales agreement), you should be able to negotiate a fixed price.

The problem is that many agents feel that they are taking on potential liability in filling out the sales agreement without getting enough compensation in return. Thus, you might need to pay the agent enough money to make it worthwhile. I've talked with agents who, reluctantly, will do the paperwork on a deal for $1,000. After all, they point out, they're exposing themselves to a possible lawsuit and they have their own errors and omissions insurance premiums to pay. In addition, state laws govern the extent to which agents/brokers can counsel you on the sales contract.

As is true with an attorney, be sure you line up a cooperating agent *before* you bring in your buyer. Be sure you've negotiated a price. One additional advantage of using an agent is that if your buyer is a *maybe* instead of a *sold,* the agent may automatically help you make the sale. (Of course, the agent may also request an additional fee for performing the sales service.)

Don'ts

We've already suggested one area that might be a minefield for you: filling out the sales agreement yourself without proper knowledge. Another is having someone who isn't really qualified do it, such as an escrow officer.

In the past, escrow officers were often obliging to sellers and buyers and would help them create a sales agreement. However, the purpose of escrow is to act as an independent third party in fulfilling the instructions of the deposit receipt. While escrow officers are normally well versed in following instructions, they may be less than adequate in creating them.

As a result, some escrow officers have painfully found themselves at the center of disputes that came about from sales agreements they helped to create. Thus, to protect themselves, today few escrow officers will help you with your sales agreement. Rather, after you have the agreement filled out and signed, they will simply aid you in seeing that its conditions are carried out.

Finally, be careful of friends who are supposedly knowledgeable in real estate and who offer to lend a helping hand. Your friend may, indeed, have successfully bought and sold a half dozen properties, but he or she may simply not have the very specific information needed for your particular transaction. That ignorance could get you in trouble.

Doing It Yourself

Okay, you've been warned about the problems. Now, how do you get it done right?

Here's a method that any FSBO owner can follow that should end up with a solid sales agreement. Be sure to follow the steps in order.

Getting to the Sales Agreement

1. *Find a buyer.* We'll have more to say about this as we move through the later chapters in this book. Here we're making the assumption that you already have the buyer and need to move forward with the paperwork.

2. *Get agreement on the terms.* Having a buyer is one thing. Having a buyer who's ready, willing and able to purchase at a price and terms for which you're willing to sell is quite something else. Probably the next most important thing after finding a buyer is coming to an agreement on price and terms. Many agents use a worksheet at this point. It includes the areas that are negotiable. By going down the worksheet and filling in the blanks, you can quickly see if you and the buyer agree on the important points as well as those you must negotiate.

3. *Take the worksheet to your attorney.* He or she should help you prepare a formal sales agreement.

4. *Sign the agreement.* Have the buyer sign it and give you a check made payable to the attorney's escrow or a licensed escrow company.
5. *Take the check and the agreement to escrow* (assuming the attorney isn't handling it), and open an escrow account. You've just passed the biggest document hurdle!

Sales Worksheet

Figure 6.1 is a worksheet that I have found to be particularly useful. Keep in mind that we're talking about a worksheet here, not a sales agreement. The purpose of this worksheet is to set down in writing all of the things that you and the buyer agree upon. *Nobody signs it.* Once you've set them down, you and the buyer can take the worksheet to an attorney or agent who can correctly fill out a sales agreement that you can sign.

Note: Getting it in writing is important. Often when two people speak, particularly two who may be in an adversarial relationship such as buyer and seller, they misunderstand each other. You may say something that the buyer misinterprets as a concession and vice versa. The whole point of doing the worksheet is that you and the buyer can sit down together and put in writing exactly what the terms of the sale are.

A Negotiation Tool

Furthermore, because neither you nor the buyer is actually going to sign this worksheet and because by itself it's not any sort of a binding agreement, it is extremely useful as a negotiating tool. There may be some point of disagreement between you and the buyer—perhaps the matter of the down payment or the interest rate on a loan you are carrying back. You can reasonably say to the buyer, "Let's sit down and see if we can work it out on paper. This is just a worksheet. I'm not going to sign it and neither are you. We'll just put the numbers down and see if we can work it out."

FIGURE 6.1

Sample FSBO Price and Terms Worksheet

Address of property _____

_____

Buyer's name _____

Seller's name _____

Price $_____

Deposit $_____

Cash down $_____

(in addition to deposit)

First mortgage $_____

	Assume _____?	New _____?
	Interest rate _____%	
	Fixed _____?	Adj. _____?
	Term _____?	Pts. _____?

Second mortgage $_____

	Assume _____?	New _____?
	Interest rate _____%	
	Fixed _____?	Adj. _____?
	Term _____?	Pts. _____?

Third mortgage $_____

	Assume _____?	New _____?
	Interest rate _____%	
	Fixed _____?	Adj. _____?
	Term _____?	Pts. _____?

Total $ _____

   (Must equal price)

FIGURE 6.1   *(Continued)*

Other conditions of sale

_____

_____

_____

_____

The date the escrow will close _____

The date the buyer gets occupancy _____

The real estate attorney to be used _____

The escrow company to be used _____

The worksheet now becomes a tool for trying out different ideas and numbers. Using the worksheet you may be able to make a deal with a buyer that you might otherwise lose. See Figure 6.1 for a sample FSBO Price and Terms Worksheet.

Understanding the Worksheet

Since the worksheet is the most important tool you have when it comes time to hammer out the price and terms, you should be clear on what it should contain. Let's take it one step at a time:

Sales Price. Most people start here and it is a good idea to at least get an offering price down. However, often the sales price comes about as the result of a combination of how much money the buyer can put down and how big a mortgage he or she can negotiate. Put down an offering price, but be sure it's in pencil so that you can scratch it out as negotiations continue.

Deposit. Sellers usually want a big deposit because they know that the bigger the deposit, the bigger the buyer's commitment to the deal. Buyers, on the other hand, often want a lower deposit, because it means they are tying up less money.

There is no rule on how big the deposit should be. It should be large enough, however, to convince you that the buyer is serious. Many agents have a hard-and-fast rule that the deposit should be $5,000, regardless of the purchase price. That hardly makes sense on lower-priced properties and may be insufficient on higher-priced ones. Here's a schedule of how big a deposit I usually want from a buyer when I am selling a house:

 Deposit Schedule

To $50,000	$1,000 minimum up to 5%
$50,000 to $100,000	$2,000 minimum up to 3%
$100,000 to $300,000	$3,000 minimum up to 3%
Over $300,000	$5,000 minimum up to 3%

Keep in mind that the deposit is what money you *may* be entitled to receive if the buyer can't complete the transaction. If the sales agreement is properly drawn and the buyer doesn't perform as promised through no fault of your own, you may get the money. In most cases, however, extenuating circumstances allow the buyer to back out of the deal and get his or her money back. Don't make the mistake of aiming for the deposit. Your goal is *not* to get the deposit, it is to sell your house.

Mortgages. This is the trickiest area for most people. If you're like most FSBO sellers, you know something, but not a great deal, about financing a real estate purchase. Thus, you may feel inadequate dealing with the issue of mortgages.

However, because virtually all real estate transactions are financed (almost no one pays cash these days), you'll have to know at least enough to get by.

We'll cover what you need to know in Chapter 10. For now, let's say that you can help the buyer by at least jotting down the amount of the mortgage(s), the estimated interest rate, points, term and type (fixed or adjustable rate).

Note: It is important that when you jot down items such as interest rate and points (points, by the way, represent percentage points of the mortgage amount—three points on a $100,000 mortgage is equal to $3,000) you list them at a *higher* level than you can reasonably expect to get at the current time. The reason is that these rates fluctuate. You don't want to lose a buyer because interest rates jumped up half a percent or points jumped between the time you hammered out the agreement and the sale was ready to close.

Terms. This, of course, is the trickiest area of all. As noted earlier, this is the area where agents got into trouble in the past. If you don't try to add a bunch of legalese, however, and leave the actual writing of the terms to your attorney or agent, you shouldn't have much of a hassle in this area.

Terms may include such items as the following:

- *How long does the buyer have to qualify for the mortgage?* You don't want to take your property off the market unless you're sure the buyer will qualify. Typically, the buyer will be entitled to a full refund of the deposit if he or she can't get the mortgage. You may want to specify that the buyer has a week to get preliminary loan approval or four weeks for final loan approval.
- *What personal property will be included in the sale?* Typically buyers will want all flooring, window covering and fixtures. You may want to specify that a favorite ceiling lamp in the dining room, for example, is not included in the sale.
- *Are there any conditions that must be met before the sale can be completed?* Buyers may want *subject to* or contingency clauses included. They may, for example, insist that the sale be subject to their recreational vehicle fitting along the side of the house. You may allow them a day or two to take measurements to be sure. On the other hand, they may insist on the sale being contingent upon the sale of their

current home. You may not want to tie up your property waiting for them to sell theirs, or you may insist that, yes, you'll give them *right of first refusal* on a sale provided that you can keep your house on the market. The term *right of first refusal* usually means that in the event you find a cash buyer before the buyers who made the first offer sell their current home, they have a set time, typically 72 hours, to remove the contingency or lose the deal.

And so forth. The terms can consist of almost anything. Your goal here is not to write them in legalese, but to get them down as clearly and succinctly as possible so that both you and the buyer know what the terms are and agree. Let the lawyer or attorney put them into formal language.

A helpful hint is to have as few terms as possible and make those few as short as possible. The more terms you have, the greater your chance of losing the deal through a misunderstanding or disagreement.

• *What inspections, if any, are you going to have?* In the past there used to be one basic inspection—for termites and fungus infestation. The reason for this inspection was that most lenders required a clearance before they would fund a mortgage.

In recent years, however, many things have changed, not the least of which are inspections. Today, it's a wise seller who *insists* that the buyer have the home inspected by a competent building inspector. Figure 6.2 lists the more frequently performed inspections.

Inspections inform the buyer of any possible defects in the property. Why, you might ask, would the seller want the buyer to know?

The reason has to do with a change in the laws in recent years in many states. In the past the buyer was at risk in a sale. It was up to the buyer to find out any defects. More recently, litigation has favored the buyer to the point that it's frequently up to the seller to disclose problems, even those problems that the seller may not know!

The result is that sellers tell buyers to have inspections. If the buyer orders the inspection, in a sense, the seller is

FIGURE 6.2

 Frequently Performed Inspections

- Foundation and basement
- Walls, ceiling, floors and structure
- Roof
- Electrical
- Plumbing
- Heating and air conditioning
- Pool and spa
- Geological
- Flood control

in a more solid position. Later on the buyer can't easily come back and claim to have been deceived by a seller who withheld information. A buyer who declines to pay for an inspection can't easily come back later, because the seller will say, "I told you to get it inspected. You chose not to; hence, you haven't got any basis to complain."

At least two states, California and Maine, now require disclosure of any defects, and it seems that others will soon follow. In any event, disclosing defects and having inspections is a good procedure for any seller. We'll have more to say on this in Chapter 12.

Note: Insisting that the buyer have inspections is also a selling feature. If you, the FSBO seller, want an inspection, most buyers will feel that you're not holding anything back.

- *State any other terms.* Everything in real estate is negotiable. Your buyer may wish to insert some strange condition that you've never heard of. If you agree to it, put it down in writing. Anything can be included. However, your real estate attorney should advise you about the wisdom of the particular terms you and the buyer want inserted.

- *Include dates.* All real estate transactions are based on performance over time. You, as the seller, should be willing to give the buyer a reasonable amount of time to arrange a loan. However, you don't want the transaction to drag on interminably. Typically, financing can be arranged in 45 days. Therefore, you will want to agree with the buyer on a date for the close of escrow and the time when the title will transfer and you'll get your sale and money.

Keep in mind that while you will agree to this date, it will be arbitrary. Things can happen that can cause delays, including financing problems on the buyer's part or, perhaps, difficulties in clearing title on your part. However, the date is what you will be aiming at. Your attorney will want to add language explaining what will happen to the deposit in the event the sale doesn't close by the appointed date or if it doesn't close at all. (See the previous section on deposits.)

The date of occupancy or when the buyer takes possession of the property is often the same date as the close of escrow, but it doesn't have to be. It can be any date you and the buyer agree upon. However, in most cases you would be wise not to let the buyer occupy the property until the deal has closed and title has transferred. The reason, simply, is that if the buyer takes possession of the property and then, for any reason, can't close the deal, you not only haven't sold your house, but you've got someone in it who you now may have to go to court to evict!

Include names. It's a good idea to name the real estate attorney, the title insurance company and the escrow company that you will be using in the transaction. Since the buyer will be filling out this form with you, you will quickly discover if he or she has any preferences. If so, you may wish to accede to them, particularly in the case of escrow and title companies. (While their fees differ slightly, most are very close in price and perform similar services.) Note:

The Real Estate Settlement Procedures Act (RESPA) may prohibit you as a seller from insisting on a particular title insurance or escrow company.

You will, however, probably want to insist on the real estate attorney (or agent) who has already agreed to write up the deal. If the buyer insists on using his or her own attorney or agent, then you may want to arrange a meeting at which both will be present, your attorney/agent and the buyer's.

In this chapter we've looked at the most important piece of documentation you will have as part of the transaction, the deposit receipt/sales agreement. Getting this document done right will help ensure a successful transaction.

CHAPTER

SEVEN

How To Find Prospects

You can't sell FSBO without working with prospective buyers (called "prospects" in the trade). Your goal is to contact as many prospects as possible and to convert at least one of them into a true purchaser. There are two parts to your task. The first is to find prospects and get them to look at your property. The second is to work with them and turn them into buyers. We'll look at how to accomplish the first task in this chapter.

Finding Prospects

At any given time there are probably at least a dozen potential buyers out there who would just love to purchase your home. If you could just get a list of them, you could send them letters, call them and even wine and dine them. They would all be interested and in a few days, chances are you would have a dozen offers.

The problem is finding just those 12. How do you distinguish them from everyone else? Consider, you may be living in a town that has 25,000 people in it or a city with 250,000 or more. How do you find just the few that will purchase your property from all the others? To get to those few people who might really be buyers for your home, you may need to wade through thousands who aren't. To put it another way, you need to get your message to as many people as possible in the hope that a few of them will be the right ones.

How do you do this? The answer is that you publicize and even advertise your property in as wide a variety of media as possible. You do whatever you can to get the word out.

This can be expensive, such as a lot of newspaper and even radio/TV advertising (which some spendthrift and desperate sellers have done in different parts of the country), or it can be inexpensive but clever. I strongly suggest going the latter route. Here are the ways you can advertise your property most effectively, yet most cheaply.

Put Out a Sign

A sign on the property is the single most effective advertising tool at your command. It lets everyone in the area know your home is for sale. (After all, how else would you discover that one of your neighbors is interested in buying?) The sign also allows anyone driving down the street to learn that your home is for sale. And when you advertise and people call and ask for directions to your property, you can simply direct them to your street and when they get close, the sign will bring them home.

There is, however, a negative to putting a sign in your front yard. It lets everyone, including those with potentially criminal intent, know that you are trying to sell. Quite frankly, some people out there look for FSBO houses and then call the owners, purporting to be interested in buying, when their real intent is to scout out the property for a potential robbery. Your best defense

FIGURE 7.1 FSBO Sign To Avoid

here is to carefully screen any potential buyers. We'll get clues on how to do this later in this chapter.

Building a Sign

Anyone can put together a sign, but it takes a bit of knowledge to build a sign that's effective, and snares potential buyers instead of shying them away. Here's what to watch for.

To begin, don't buy a ready-made sign at the store for a couple of dollars that says "For Sale by Owner" and gives you a place in which to write in your phone number (see Figure 7.1).

These cheap, ready-made signs look just that, cheap. Potential buyers driving by are likely to think that you are a rank amateur, may not be very serious and probably don't know much about what you are doing. After all, if you're not even willing to get a decent sign, how committed are you actually to selling the property?

Get a professionally made sign. These may cost you 50 bucks apiece, but they look good, they catch attention and they say that you're a committed seller and know what you're about. How do you know a good sign? It will look just like an agent's sign. It will be roughly the same size (20 inches by 30 inches), the lettering will be clear and in a color readily seen, such as red, and it will be well designed and not look amateurish. The sign should also contain vital information (see Figures 7.2 and 7.3).

FIGURE 7.2   Information To Place an FSBO Sign

FOR SALE

Builders, landscapers and politicians put signs in yards. You want people to know that in your case, it's the house that's for sale. These words and your phone number should be the largest elements.

BY OWNER

This may be your best selling point. It doesn't have to be large, but it should be prominent.

BEDS/BATHS

I always suggest that you list how many bedrooms and bathrooms your house has. Many buyers are looking for certain sizes. For example, yours may be a four-bedroom, three-bath house. This is a plus. (If you have only two bedrooms—a minus—you may want to leave this fact off the sign.)

ONE SPECIAL FEATURE

You don't really have room for more than one. Typically you might say, "Pool" or "Spa" or "Large Yard." Often this can be attached as a separate, smaller part of the sign.

SHOWN BY APPOINTMENT

This is an important part of your sign. Without it, you will have people knocking at your door constantly. You may still have some of these. But, hopefully, most people will call first and you can screen them before admitting them to your home.

PHONE NUMBER

This must be large and clear. Use sans serif type. It's easiest to read.

FIGURE 7.3 More Effective FSBO Sign

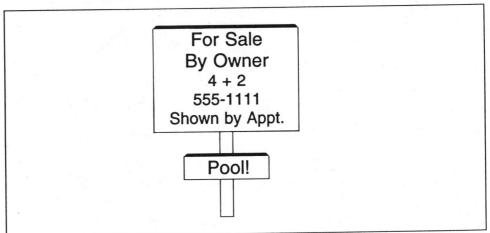

Where Do You Put the Sign?

Placement of the sign is important. It should be clearly visible from cars traveling both ways on the street. If necessary, particularly for corner lots, you may need to post separate signs, one at each end of the property. Often, you may want to have two signs back-to-back placed in the front of your property.

A sign parallel to the house might be difficult to see except when someone is right in front. A double sign placed perpendicular to the house can be read easily by people in cars as they drive by.

A word of caution: Some cities restrict the kind of sign you may put on your home. Check with your local zoning department. Many condominium associations prohibit owners from putting signs in their front yard. You may be limited, in this case, to a small sign in a window.

Use an Information Box

The sign is an attention-getter, but by itself, it isn't going to hook a prospect. It may cause them to slow down, look at your home and jot down the phone number. The problem is that they

FIGURE 7.4   Sample Information Box

may not have a pen handy or a piece of paper, or the whole thing may seem like too much hassle at the time.

A prospect needs more information. Many good agents have recently taken to hanging an information box just below the "For Sale" sign. The information box contains copies of a leaflet that gives much more detailed information on the property. It answers some of the potential buyers' questions as well as whets their appetites to see the house. The leaflet is actually a great marketing tool and I urge you to use it (see Figure 7.4).

You can easily build the information box yourself. All that you need is a small wood or metal box that will shed water and keep direct sunlight away. (The sunlight tends to fade whatever's written on your leaflets.) Hang the box on the post holding the sign and label it "For More Information" or "Free Leaflet" or "Free, Take One."

Potential buyers will get the idea. They'll stop the car, get out and pick up the leaflet. Instantly they have a host of information about your home.

Information To Give To Prospects

It's a good idea to be careful about what you put in and leave out of the leaflet. It may be the very item that will make a buyer really enthusiastic about your property. If this sheet is done properly, it will give all the information a buyer really needs to decide

FIGURE 7.5

✏️ **Information Leaflet**

_____

Buyer's guide to (address goes here) _____

Price _____

Seller's name _____

Grammar school _____

Intermediate school _____

High school _____

# of Bedrooms _____

# of Baths _____

Size of garage (1-, 2- or 3-car)

Air-conditioned? _____

Pool or spa? _____

Lot size _____ × _____

Age _____

Special features:_____

Photo (color, if possible) of your house

Your phone number (large) goes here

---

that your home is one that he or she may want to look at further
(see Figure 7.5).

Be careful—you don't want to include too much information.
For example, never include specific financial information such as
your existing mortgages. Don't put down what you originally

paid for the property. These sorts of things may come up later, but they shouldn't be the first thing that a buyer sees.

Always include a photo of your house. The old adage "a picture is worth a thousand words" applies here. Just being able to see your house often will allow a potential buyer to determine whether or not your place is in the running. You don't have to be a professional photographer (or hire one) to take the picture. Any point-and-shoot camera will do. Try to take the picture on a day that is overcast. The house will come out quite clearly. If you take the shot in bright sunlight, you'll end up with too many shadows.

The information leaflet in Figure 7.5 won't cost all that much to produce. You can handle the typing yourself and get the sheet reproduced for about a nickel a page at most copy centers. A 4-inch by 6-inch photo is more expensive, but it still can be produced for between a quarter and half a dollar apiece if ordered in quantities.

Spread the Information Around

Once you've got this leaflet, it would be a shame not to go around and pin it up at a wide variety of other places where potential buyers might stop by. Some suggestions are provided below.

- Housing offices: Schools, military installations and larger corporations often operate housing offices for their people to help them find places to live. Often these people are looking to buy. I suggest that you contact any place near your home (within a 10-mile to 15-mile radius) and ask the staff if you can hang your leaflet in the office. Most of the time they will be happy to have you do this. (While you can call and then send in the leaflet, my suggestion is that you actually stop by. That way you'll know that it actually gets hung up.)
- Bulletin boards: Shopping centers, stores, libraries, civic centers, public buildings and other areas often have a public bulletin board. Don't be shy about hanging your leaflet up. Just keep in mind that you will have to go back

every couple of weeks to be sure it's still hanging there. (Sometimes it's a good idea to attach a half dozen small Post-its to the bottom of your sheet with your address and phone number so that anyone interested can take this information. Otherwise, they will tend simply to rip down the leaflet.)

Advertising

Publicity is what we've considered thus far, getting the information out for free. Yes, it will cost you for a sign and a leaflet, but after that the publicity doesn't cost anything.

Unfortunately, to reach the largest number of people in a reasonable amount of time, you will probably have to go one step better: to paid advertising. This usually takes the form of your local newspaper.

Newspaper Ads

The trouble with newspaper ads is that they are so expensive. If your paper has even a modest circulation, it can easily cost you $25 a week for a tiny ad and much more for an ad in which you can elaborate on your home. Nevertheless, to get the word out, you can't afford to miss this important medium.

My suggestion is that you try both kinds of ads, the little inexpensive ones and the bigger, more descriptive ads. (We'll look at examples of both in a few paragraphs.) You may want to alternate ads on different weeks. One word of caution: Never run the same ad for more than a week. When potential buyers see the same ad run over a longer period of time they begin to recognize it and often think of it as that house that still hasn't sold. You don't want readers to think of your house as stale on the market, but as fresh. Hence, my suggestion is that you create a number of different ads and rotate them.

Also, you may find that you have a choice of where to place your ad. In my community there are one major and two local paid newspapers plus at least three flyers that are delivered free around town. All accept paid advertising. Obviously, I can't advertise in all six, as it would be prohibitively expensive.

Therefore, I suggest that you do what I do, which is to borrow the marketing savvy of those whose business it is to know which papers get the most attention. I get a couple of copies of each and then see which ones carry the most real estate advertising, particularly advertising by agents whose livelihood depends on knowing how to get the most out of their advertising dollar. Typically, one or maybe two newspapers or flyers will carry a significantly larger number of ads for homes than the others. That's the one I would use for my own ad and I suggest you do likewise. Of course, if after a couple of tries you get poor results, you can always switch to a different paper.

Small Ads

The small ad has only the most meager ingredients. It usually includes the following, reads as one long sentence and is often heavily abbreviated.

Figure 7.6 shows the basics you need to cover in an ad. Figure 7.7 is a typical example of a short, yet effective, advertisement. The ad itself can vary enormously, but you're simply not going to get a whole lot into just three to five lines.

As long as you include the basics: FSBO, price, location, size, best feature(s), inducement and phone number you've done your best. By the way, many sellers, particularly those old-timers who have done this many times, swear by this small ad. They say that real buyers comb the newspapers and look especially for the tiny ads by owner. They claim that these small ads often get twice the response of much larger ads. My own experience tends to confirm this.

One final word about the lead. The expression "for sale by owner" is one of the biggest selling features. Buyers know that they may have already seen properties advertised by agents (because of their cooperation through listing services). However, if it's by owner, unless they've been to your house, chances are they haven't seen it.

FIGURE 7.6　The Basics To Cover in an Ad

1. **FSBO**—Usually this means the ad starts with the words "By Owner."

2. **The Price**—Buyers shop by price. If your house is $100,000, you're wasting your time with buyers who are looking for $50,000 or $300,000 homes.

3. **Location**—Buyers within a price range always shop location. You needn't give out your street address. Just give the tract or the area of town.

4. **Size**—Typically this means the number of bedrooms and bathrooms.

5. **Best Selling Feature**—It could be a large lot or a pool/spa or the fact that it's redecorated or has an extra room or some other attribute.

6. **Inducements**—Here I mean words indicating that you are eager to sell or that this is an especially good buy or some other reason that will motivate a buyer to call.

7. **Phone Number**—Forget this and the ad's a waste.

Of course, you may want to switch and stick the most important feature as the lead. It could be the size, the location, the features, anything. Just be sure that somewhere in the ad you also include the fact that you're selling FSBO.

Larger Ads

As your ad gets larger (and more expensive) you can afford to expand on the features of what you're selling. However, you want to be sure that you don't waste space (and money). What you say should be the most powerful inducement possible to snag buyers.

To accomplish this I suggest you limit each ad to a single positive theme; that is, to point out how your house is different, and a better deal, than other homes on the market. You have to

FIGURE 7.7   Example of a Short, Yet Effective Ad

BY OWNER·

$105,000 split-level, Shadow Hills, 3 + 2, pool, large lot, anxious, make offer, 555-1234.
---

identify what makes your home outstanding. Figure 7.8 shows you some of the more likely attributes.

Writing an Ad That Pulls

Large corporations spend billions of dollars annually to come up with catchy advertising that will sell products. Hence, you may think, what chance do you have of writing a winning ad for your home?

Your chances, actually, are excellent. The reason is that you don't need to create an advertising campaign or write a hundred words of great copy. You need only two or three good ads to alternate in the newspaper. Further, you can save a couple of Sunday papers (when the real estate advertising is heavy), note those ads by agents that catch your attention and build your ad around them. They say that copying is the sincerest form of flattery, and while I don't suggest you copy someone else's ad verbatim, you can borrow the idea without any problem. Another bit of wisdom is that there's nothing new under the sun, which means that the ads you see were probably themselves based on and taken from other advertising.

As noted above, it is important to get across the main theme in your ad. Therefore, I've included a number of ideas, all of which are based on actual ads taken from several newspapers over a period of a few weeks. By the way, you may want to vary the theme of your ad from week to week. If you find that pushing the size of your property doesn't work, you may want to push the low down payment or reduced price. At different times, buyers

FIGURE 7.8   What Makes Your Home Better?

- Good price
- Owner-assisted financing/Low down/Low payments
- Great location
- Larger size than . . . .
- More room (bigger lot, more bedrooms)
- Unusual features

respond to different incentives (depending on the economy, market conditions, what's available, etc.).

The Price Ad

The incentive here is that your price is lower in some way. If you can say that yours is the lowest-priced three-bedroom, two-bath home in your tract, it's a great come-on. Just be sure it's true. A safer tactic can be to advertise your price outright or, as in Figure 7.9, emphasize that your price is lower than it was before.

Of course, also keep in mind that while your theme is what may catch a reader's eye, it's all of the other features that will convince that reader to make the call. Figure 7.10 is another example of a price ad.

FIGURE 7.9   Sample Price Ad

REDUCED!

For quick sale—Split-level with fireplace, great area close to top schools, manicured lot, recently painted, new carpeting, 4 + 2 with FR. Make offer and move in before summer's over! By owner $89,950, 555-2345.

FIGURE 7.10   Sample Price Ad (2)

> **SELLER DESPERATE!**
>
> Must sell, make offer. Top location, four large bedrooms with bonus room over garage. Formal dining room with wet bar in den. Lender is threatening, see now. $179,950 by owner. 555-2211.

The Low-Down or Better Financing Ad

Here your goal is to attract buyers who don't have enough cash to purchase a house in the normal way. Your advertising must emphasize the financial aspects. The buyer can get in with a lower-than-normal down payment, lower monthly payments or greater ease in qualifying for a mortgage (see Figure 7.11).

Remember, always put the theme of your ad into the lead. The first line, or lead, is what catches attention. If it's something that readers want, they will read on with interest. Otherwise, they'll just skim past it. Also, remember that each time you emphasize one aspect of your property or financing, you downplay another. If you point out the wonderfully low down payment, as in Figure 7.11, a buyer with enough money down, but who needs easy qualifying for a mortgage, may skip right over it. That's why I suggest several ads that run on alternating weeks, each emphasizing a different theme.

Note that when you're advertising the financing, sometimes it isn't necessary to include the price. After all, a potential buyer has all the necessary information in this ad, *if* he or she is looking

FIGURE 7.11   Sample Low Down Payment Ad

> **LOW DOWN PAYMENT!**
>
> Only $3,000 moves you in! Seller will carry 15 percent second at reduced interest rate. Hurry, won't last long. Two-bed adult condo, $67K by owner, 555-5123.

FIGURE 7.12   Sample Financing Ad

ASSUMABLE LOAN!

FHA fully assumable 6½%. Pmts. only $837 per month. Seller will consider financing part of down. Choice location; must sell by April 1 or lose! Come see, make offer today. By owner— 555-6789.

---

for easy qualifying (assumability, interest rate and monthly payment). Often a fully assumable loan at a good interest rate will allow the seller to get a better price, assuming that it's an unusual situation for the market (see Figure 7.12).

Be careful of advertising something that is commonly available. In the Phoenix market, for example, virtually every other inexpensive house used to have an assumable loan, so emphasizing that won't impress too many buyers.

The House with Amenities

In some areas and in some markets, it's not price or down payment that sells; it's what the house itself has to offer. This is particularly the case if your home is in a more exclusive area.

In Figure 7.13, the owner is emphasizing all the special amenities of this house. Presumably, buyers in this price range are looking for features, rather than terms and price. (This isn't always the case; most of the time buyers are concerned about price and terms as well. But all things being equal, amenities will sell.)

The ad in Figure 7.13 was taken from a paper near San Francisco (where prices are the highest in the country). While the house must be nice, the advertisement actually wastes the owner's money. In this price range and suburb one would expect hardwood floors, air conditioning, three-car garage and good location. Mentioning this isn't going to impress the reader.

Furthermore, the phrase "must see to appreciate" is frequently found in real estate agent ads and is often used to

FIGURE 7.13   Sample Features Ad That Doesn't Work

EXECUTIVE MANSION!

Big 5 + 4 with lighted tennis court. Solid wood throughout, oak floors, air, 2-story, pool with spa, gardenlike setting, secluded, 3-car garage, choice location, has it all—must see to appreciate $655K, For Sale By Owner—555-5551.

---

describe a property that's really in a poor location. Hence, repeating it here is likely to make potential buyers wary. The ad would do far better to emphasize features truly exclusive to this house.

The ad in Figure 7.14 has two fewer lines than the one preceding it, yet it has more of the specifics that appeal to the kind of buyer the seller wants to attract. The rule here is that when in doubt, be as specific as possible.

One point to reemphasize: don't put the address in the ad. The address not only lets potential buyers know where the house is; it also lets those with robbery on their minds know. Let the buyers call. Screen them on the phone. Then arrange for a time to show the property when you know you'll be there. More about this is discussed in later chapters.

The Bigger Than Ad

Sometimes what makes your house special is its size, or the size of the lot. If so, you need to get that information to the reader. Once again, however, remember that you may have the

FIGURE 7.14   Sample Features Ad That Does Work

EXECUTIVE MANSION!

Huge 5 + 4 with two-story view of Mt. Diablo, wine cellar, pool/spa, lighted tennis court, secluded, in-town location, one-of-a-kind $655K, For Sale By Owner—555-5551.

FIGURE 7.15   Another Sample Features Ad That Doesn't Work

ROOM TO ROAM

A full 1/3 acre with 11 mature fruit trees. Zoned for horse lover, includes barn with new roof. Low maintenance/low water irrigation system. Ranch house with in/out gas barbecue, over 2,600 usable ft. of space. Circular drive and more. $319,950, FSBO—Call 555-5432

---

biggest house or lot in town, but if the price and terms are wrong, it probably still won't sell. Just having a big yard or home isn't by itself necessarily all that wonderful.

In Figure 7.15, an ad taken from a Los Angeles paper, the seller is pointing out that the one-third acre has fruit trees and a barn, in case a horse owner is looking for property. In other words, it isn't just space, but is usable space.

The drawback here is that one-third acre is probably too small for horse raising and fruit trees, and this fact won't be lost on a potential buyer. You can't really advertise that you have room for horses unless you are selling a pasture.

The Unusual Feature

Finally, there's the ad that offers a special feature. It could be an indoor grill, an added-on playroom, a special decor or, as in Figure 7.16, the location of the property.

FIGURE 7.16   Unusual Feature Ad

LOCATION, LOCATION, LOCATION!

It's everything and this home has it all located next to top shopping and transportation in the heart of the desirable Westlake area. 3 + 2 with wet bar, spa and RV parking. $150K by owner. Call 555-1122.

Caution: Many owners feel that their property is well located when, compared with other properties, it isn't. My suggestion is that you ask several agents to name the best feature of your home. They can often point out whether it's really location or something else.

Advertising Elsewhere

A variety of other avenues of advertising may be open to you. The most promising new medium is cable television. Most cable systems have a public access channel that is open to a wide variety of local programming.

Often they will run a commercial for a product, say your house, for a nominal fee to cover setup costs. The fees are typically under $50 and often around $25. You can prepare a short commercial of, for example, 30 seconds using a home camcorder. You can show the front, back and inside of your home as well as describe the price, terms and attributes. (It's really amazing what you can get into a 30-second slot.)

I urge you to try this avenue. Keep in mind that the only people who are likely to watch and listen to this sort of commercial are buyers, but, after all, who are you looking to attract?

Talking Up Your House

Finally, there's the old tried-and-true method of talking up your property. How many people do you come in contact with in a day, a week? If you're working and socially active, the number could actually be in the hundreds. My suggestion is that you bring up the subject of your home for sale with everyone you meet. Talk to your coworkers, especially your neighbors, the lunch counter cook, your friends, everyone and anyone.

You never know who's looking to buy a house. A few of the people to whom you talk, if they aren't in the market themselves, may know others who are. Think of it as starting a rumor. It

FIGURE 7.17

✏️ **Getting the Word Out Worksheet**

_____

1. Sign (visible from both directions) _____
2. Information box _____
3. Information leaflet (or pass out) _____
4. Distribute leaflet at:
   - Housing offices _____
   - Bulletin boards _____
   - Shopping centers _____
   - Malls _____
   - Schools _____
5. Short newspaper ads _____
6. Longer ads _____

---

expands as it goes, reaching more and more people. Eventually, it may catch the ear of just the right buyer for your home.

Worksheet for Finding Prospects

The worksheet in Figure 7.17 is intended both as a review and a checklist. It gives you the potential sources for finding prospects for your FSBO. You aren't finished advertising your property until you've got a check in each column. Don't forget the less formal technique of informing friends, relatives and coworkers that your house is for sale.

CHAPTER EIGHT

Converting Lookers to Buyers

One of the first things you'll discover as soon as you put your house up for sale as a FSBO is that you get a large number of lookers coming by. These are people who call up, make an appointment, then come by and look at this, look at that, say a few words and depart, often never to be heard from again. What's important to understand is that hidden amongst these lookers are probably more than a few buyers. Your goal is to identify the buyers and make a sale.

In this chapter we're going to discuss how to deal with lookers who come buy, how to convert them to buyers and then how to clinch a sale.

Selling

I've always maintained that the product, in this case the house, either sells itself or it doesn't. Thus, assuming you've fixed up your property as described in Chapter 9, when it comes to selling, your job is largely informational. You need to be sure that the potential looker is informed of all of the features and advantages of the home.

This doesn't mean that you spend a lot of time talking off the looker's ear. Often a sale can be lost because the salesperson talks so much that the potential buyer never gets a chance to really see the house and finally leaves rather than listen anymore. What's needed is getting prospects in, letting them look around and being ready to answer any questions. We'll have more to say about this shortly. First, let's consider just how to deal with lookers at first contact, which usually means the initial phone call.

Answering the Phone

It's important at the outset, vital even, to understand that when you're selling your home, it's at the buyer's convenience, not yours. I think the analogy of fishing is helpful: when you go fishing, it's not the fish's responsibility to get on your hook; it's up to you to have that hook in the water, properly baited and waiting for as long as it takes to get a nibble.

The same holds true for selling your home. It's not the buyer's responsibility to keep calling you repeatedly until he or she finally finds you at home. It's up to you to be sure that every phone call is promptly answered, that information is provided and that you at least get the caller's name and phone number.

What this means is that as soon as you put your house up for sale by owner with your phone number on your sign, leaflets and advertising, your phone must never be unattended. It's going to take a little extra effort and, perhaps, a couple of bucks, but being sure that the phone is always answered is the first step in hooking a buyer. Ideally, you would be home 24 hours a day,

FIGURE 8.1   Typical Answering Machine Message

"You've reached the Smith home. Yes, it's for sale and, yes, we'd love to show it to you. The price is $95,000, we offer excellent seller financing, the house is large with four bedrooms and two baths and is recently redecorated. Please leave your name and number and we'll call you back as soon as possible to make an appointment to show it."

ready to answer any buyer's questions. Obviously, that's not going to happen. So what's next best?

Using an Answering Machine

An answering machine with the proper message can cover for you somewhat. (It's not as good as a real live person, but it's probably second best.) I suggest that you use a message like the one in Figure 8.1.

I can recite this message easily within 15 seconds, which is the time most answering machines provide for outgoing messages. The message itself tends to be buoyant, informative and has just enough of a hook to get potential buyers to leave their names and phone numbers.

A word of caution: Since one of your goals is to get the caller's name and number, some sellers are inclined to use only an answering machine. That way, they feel they are sure to get that caller's name and number even before they begin a conversation.

Bad move.

Many buyers, sincere buyers, don't want to leave a name and number. They don't want to be bothered by sellers who may be desperate and may make pests of themselves by repeatedly calling back. The answering machine is only second best to answering the call yourself. Use it only if you can't be there. Note that most local phone companies offer call forwarding. If you're going to be available at another location near a phone, consider this option. It is relatively inexpensive and it might make a big difference.

A Designated Answerer

The third least desirable alternative, to my way of thinking, is having another family member answer the phone. Sometimes this is inevitable, as when a potential buyer or seller calls in the evening and your son or daughter picks up the phone.

Be sure to cue everyone that if a call is about the house, it should go to you immediately. If you're not there, instruct whoever answers the phone to get only the name and number for you to call back. If a another person begins giving out information about your house, they may blow it. They may present the information in such a way that a buyer gets turned off or decides too hastily that this place is not for her.

The worst scenario is a child answering the phone. Even if the child is a teenager, they may turn the buyer off unless they are very comfortable responding to phone messages and know exactly what to say.

The best situation is having a designated answerer—you, your spouse or someone else. If a buyer calls and anyone else picks up the phone, the caller should be quickly transferred to that designated person. If the designated answerer isn't home, whoever answered takes a simple message—name and phone number. It's clear cut and leaves little room for error.

A Dedicated Phone Line

Finally, consider putting in a separate phone line during the time you have your home for sale. The line would be dedicated strictly to calls on the house. All of your advertising (sign, leaflets, etc.) would give that number only. When that dedicated phone line rings, you know that it is someone inquiring about the house.

Yes, a separate line costs a few dollars more, but if you're really sincere about selling your house, it could be well worth the added expense.

FIGURE 8.2

✐ Phone Report

1. What is your name? _____

2. What is your phone number? _____

3. What is your work phone number in case I can't catch you at home? _____

4. Are you a local resident? _____

5. Where do you live? (What part of town) _____

   _____

6. Are you an out-of-towner? _____

7. Where are you staying locally? _____

8. Currently own a house?   _____

9. Is current house sold?   _____

10. Is it listed or FSBO?   _____

11. When do you plan to sell and move?   _____

12. What is your monthly or annual income?   _____

The Phone Report

The purpose of the phone report is threefold (see Figure 8.2). First, it identifies the caller and gives you his or her phone number plus other information to help you determine if you want to show your home to this person. (When you are selling FSBO, your security must always be a consideration.) Second, getting the phone number means that you can call the party back at a later date to ask how the house hunting is coming along and perhaps rekindle interest in your place. Third, it is the first step in helping you to qualify a potential buyer. After you've talked for awhile, the buyer may provide enough information for you to determine whether he or she has sufficient income and strong enough credit to purchase your home.

Asking Questions

It's important to understand that when a potential buyer calls you don't begin the conversation by asking the questions on the phone report (although a family member who's taking a message might do just that with at least the caller's name and phone number). When you, the seller, get a phone response to an ad, your sign or some other source, you should first describe your home.

Describe how it looks, how big it is, how good the location is and so forth. You should give the potential buyer information. I don't mean that you should just jabber on and on. Listen carefully to what the caller says and try to answer questions honestly and completely.

For the buyers, the first part of the conversation is always a matter of determining whether your house is even remotely close to what they are looking for. Buyers will ask about the price, size, special terms and, most important, location. If the conversation goes on for awhile and the buyer seems interested, then you can offer to show the house. If the caller agrees, then you are perfectly within your rights to ask for a name, phone number and other such information. I suggest that the questions be asked informally, as if you're just curious (which you are), not as if you're an inquisitor.

The first seven questions listed in Figure 8.2 are pretty straightforward, and most potential buyers won't usually hesitate to answer them. After all, if they're going to come and see your house, they can understand your interest in learning a little bit about them. Questions 8 through 12 are a bit trickier. They involve specific questions that will help you determine if this is a real buyer with whom you should spend time or just a looker.

If the caller already owns a house he or she is living in, hasn't sold it and hasn't even put it up for sale, you're not dealing with a buyer. This person is months away from being able to buy. You may want to get the number and call back a couple of months later (if your house is still for sale) to see if he or she is closer to selling the current home.

Question 12 is the trickiest of all. This information is important to you because it tells you pretty closely whether or not the caller can qualify to purchase your home. The trouble is that most people aren't willing to disclose this information, at least over the phone. My suggestion is that you don't ask this question at all unless you've established a good rapport with the caller. Then, ask it only if the subject of qualifying for your home comes up in the course of conversation.

For example, the caller might say something such as, "Your price seems rather high. I don't know if we can afford that much." To which you might reply, "Well, how much do you make? I can quickly tell you if it's enough for a loan." And so forth.

Keep one thing in mind: because you're a FSBO seller, the caller is going to be just a bit wary of confiding too much in you. After all, you're the person that caller is going to have to negotiate with if he or she decides to buy. Therefore, don't push too hard. If the caller hesitates and doesn't want to answer, let it go.

The only information you absolutely need is the caller's name, phone number and address, and that's mainly for security reasons. Although this system does not ensure that the caller is a prospective buyer and not a robber, it gives you the chance to call back and confirm your appointment before allowing anyone into your home.

Setting Up Appointments

Remember the fishing story at the beginning of this chapter? Well, it applies to showing your house just as it does to answering the phone. When you've got your home for sale, you must make it available when a potential buyer wants to see it, not necessarily when it's convenient for you. If someone calls and wants to see it at four in the afternoon and you had planned on playing bridge this afternoon, cancel bridge and show the house. If a buyer calls at seven in the morning and wants to see the house at eight, if you're convinced he or she is a serious buyer, show it.

For safety reasons some wary sellers make it a rule never to show their homes at night.

This means that your home must be ready for showing almost anytime, and you must bend over backward to make time for buyers to see the place.

If you think this is a royal pain, you're right. It's inconvenient for you. It's imposing on you. It's downright frustrating. It's also necessary if you want to sell your home. A serious buyer is looking not only at your house but also at many other houses. If your home isn't available to see, that buyer will see another one and possibly buy it instead of yours.

By Appointment Only

My suggestion is that you hang a small sign onto your big FSBO sign (as well as attach a small note to your flyer) that says, "Shown By Appointment Only."

There are many reasons for this stipulation. First, it means potential buyers should call before coming by, which gives you a chance to get names and phone numbers. It also gives you a chance to determine if prospects are legitimate and qualified.

Drop-Ins

No matter how much you indicate the house will be shown by appointment only, people will knock on the door and ask to see it right then. Be careful, but try not to turn them down.

Frequently buyers cruise neighborhoods in which they are interested. They see your sign and think, maybe your house is a possibility. Yes, it's shown by appointment only, but they don't have time to come back, or so they think. So, they knock and ask if they can see it now. Chances are that they are serious buyers and you would risk losing a potential sale by not showing it.

On the other hand, drop-ins are totally unscreened. You don't know anything about them and you could be putting your-

FIGURE 8.3   Rules for Screening Potential Buyers

1. Before letting people in, get them to write down their names, addresses and phone numbers. Serious buyers shouldn't hesitate to do this. At least confirm this in your phone book.

2. Ask questions such as those on the Phone Report (see Figure 8.2).

3. Never let *any* drop-in into your house after dark. It's just too dangerous in the times in which we live. If it's a weekend in the afternoon and lots of people are around and about, you can consider it.

4. Never show the property when you are alone, particularly if you are a woman. Simply explain that it is an inconvenient time and offer to set up an appointment.

   Yes, this may mean a potential buyer will get away. But the risk is simply too great. Think of it this way: If your house were not up for sale, would you let in anyone who knocked on the door? The rules don't change that much when it is FSBO.

self at risk by letting them in. Figure 8.3 presents my suggestions for showing the property to drop-ins.

Showing the Home

Once you've determined that you have a potential buyer and not just another looker, the showing of the home is your next task. When you're setting up the appointment, try to leave yourself at least an hour, if possible. The reason is simple. You're going to have to do an awful lot of preparation before that potential buyer arrives at your FSBO. Figure 8.4 explains the rules to help you prepare the house for showing.

FIGURE 8.4

☑ **Rules for Preparing the House for Showing**

1. *Before* the buyer arrives, be sure that your home is neat and clean. This includes:

   • Vacuum carpets.   Done? _____

   • Sweep hallways.   Done? _____

   • Wash kitchen and bath floors.   Done? _____

   • Scrub sinks, toilets, tubs and showers.   Done? _____

   • Wash and put away all dirty dishes.   Done? _____

   • Be sure countertops are clean, neat and mostly empty.   Done? _____

   • Put away all loose clothing.   Done? _____

   • Make all beds.   Done? _____

2. *Before* the buyer arrives, be sure that you go around and turn on ALL the lights in the house. Even if it's the middle of the day, turn on all the lights. Buyers like homes that are light and airy, so having lots of lights on helps with this. Open all curtains and window shades as well.   Done? _____

3. *Before* the buyer arrives, check the odors in the house. Bathroom odors will offend most buyers. Use fresheners. Some clever sellers will even have a pot boiling on the stove containing aromatic herbs or cookies baking in the oven, thus giving the house a warm, homey feel.   Done? _____

FIGURE 8.4   *(Continued)*

4. *Before* the buyer arrives, check the noise level. If there's no disturbing outside or inside noise, you're okay. If there are disturbing noises, such as someone working on the street, try turning on the stereo to a calm station. Be careful of playing rock and roll or other loud music. It may offend some buyers' tastes. (I don't suggest always turning on the stereo, as some agents do, because having low music on sometimes suggests to buyers that the scene has been artificially set. But if there's noise outside, then maybe even an artificially set scene is better.)   Done? _____

5. *Before* the buyer arrives, if it's in winter, light a fire in the fireplace so the house will feel warm and cozy. On an especially cold day turn up the heat. If it's summer, be sure that the air conditioning (if you have it) is working and lower the temperature. You want the buyer to feel comfortable. (Note: An old trick that car salespeople use is to always turn on the car's air-conditioning in a test drive. Marketing studies have shown that buyers are far more inclined to move positively when the temperature is just below 70 degrees!)   Done? _____

Security

As noted earlier, you may want to have a second person with you for security when you show the home. Also, it's usually a good idea to keep the curtains open so that people from outside can easily see what's going on inside.

Then there's the matter of your valuables. Never, never leave valuables in the home when you're showing. (That includes inside drawers.) Put them in a safety deposit box. Drop them off with friends or relatives. The rule is simple, if you don't leave something around that a person can walk off with, it won't get stolen. By the way, this applies whether you're selling by FSBO or with an agent.

When the Potential Buyers Arrive

Greet all buyers warmly and ask friendly questions, such as, "Did you have any trouble finding the house?" (if they called on an ad) or, "How did you happen to hear of our house?"

Another good starting point is to ask if the potential buyers have ever purchased a home from a FSBO. Chances are they haven't, so you can start up a conversation by pointing out that you're selling by owner to get a quick sale. You can note that one of the big benefits to a buyer of your not having to pay a full commission is a lower sales price. (Be sure, of course, that you do, in fact, have a lower sales price. See Chapter 5 for information on pricing.)

Once the buyers get into the house and you've established a rapport with them, think of the rule for showing:

 Rule for Showing Your House

Get out of the buyers' way.

There's only one rule here, but it's important. It's like the old story about a thirsty horse: "You can lead a horse to water, but you can't make it drink."

The same applies to buyers. You can get them into your house, but you can't make them buy. The very worst thing you can do is point out every darling little nook and cranny, every precious thing that you have in your house.

Most buyers hate a pushy salesperson, and when that salesperson is the seller, they doubly hate it. The very best thing you can do, after welcoming them to your house and establishing rapport, is to get out of their way. Yes, you can walk around with them (to be sure they don't take anything), but it's best if you let them wander through your house and see it for themselves. (Remember, you should have removed valuables long before you let a prospect into your home. Remove them from inside drawers as well.)

Wise sellers will often go out into the yard or the garage so that the buyers can be by themselves. Your goal is getting the buyers to feel comfortable in your home. They need to feel that they could live in your house and make it their own. They can't possibly do that if you stand next to them and keep pointing out ways that you've made the house your own.

There are two concerns here. The first, as we've already seen, is security. Leaving buyers alone in the house means that they can, possibly, take something of value while you're not there to notice. After all, even the most seemingly trustworthy buyers could still turn out to be crooks. You really don't know who these people are.

The second concern is that the buyers will overlook something important. For example, you may have oak wood floors, an important selling feature, but if the floors are covered with carpet, the buyers may not notice.

Yes, they may ask, but you should be ready to tell them in any case. You can address this situation in two ways. I suggest doing both. When the buyers first come in, hand them a sheet (which you've already prepared) describing all the best features of the house. (See Chapter 7 for what to include.) They can read the sheet as they walk through the house.

Second, when the potential buyers have had some time to walk through and look at the house (you can tell because they start coming out), it's a good idea to pop in and point out all the best features of your home. You may begin with a comment such as, "Did you notice that we have all hardwood oak floors under the carpet?" or, "Did you see the fireplace in the master bedroom?"

You get the idea. You're simply giving the buyers information on features that they may have missed. Very often it will turn out that the buyers didn't really see all of the special features of your house and if they are interested, they may want to go back and look again. Accompany them this time and point out those features.

This is also a good time to begin a conversation about other concerns the potential buyers may have. You can talk about the proximity to schools and shopping. Buyers may want to know about the quality of the local schools as well as about the neighborhood and, in particular, your neighbors.

You can also talk about financing and any special terms you are offering. You may need to help the buyers understand how financing works.

In general, what you want is to be helpful. You want to give the buyers as much accurate information as possible.

One further point. Get time on your side. The longer the potential buyers hang around talking to you, the more they have invested in the house (in terms of time and commitment). If you can get potential buyers to stick around for an hour, you may get yourself a sale. On the other hand, don't give up on buyers just because they quickly walk through and leave. They may have another appointment. However, when you call back later, you may find out that they really did like your house. (We'll talk about the callback shortly.)

Trying To Close the Deal Too Soon

Most of us would like to have the potential buyers walk through, ask a few questions and then say, "We'll take it!"

It isn't likely to happen that way, at least not on this planet. Very few buyers will walk in, look at your house and then agree to purchase. (The exception here is the buyers who have been looking at a lot of homes, have made up their minds on exactly what they want and have determined quickly that your house fits their bill. It could happen, but you could grow old and gray waiting for such a deal to drop out of heaven.)

What's more likely to happen is that the buyers will spend some time looking at the house and talking with you, then leave. Perhaps a few days later, they will call (or you'll call them) and want to see it again. Buyers may need to see the house several times before actually deciding that they want to buy. That's far more likely to be the scenario.

Therefore, it's important that you don't try to close on the first showing. The seller who lets the buyers walk through and then says, "Okay, let's draw up the deal," appears naive, puts the buyers on the spot and could lose the sale. *Don't appear to be pressuring the buyers*. Doing so would only backfire.

Wait until the buyers call back or until you call them. Then you can ask a few questions to determine if they are really interested.

Holding an Open House

Real estate agents are always holding open houses. They seem to be a backbone of home sales. If it works for agents, will it work for you? Should you as a FSBO seller hold your own open house?

No . . . and yes.

First, let's understand what an agent hopes to accomplish with an open house. Numerous studies have clearly shown that almost never does a buyer who comes to an open house actually buy that particular house.

This does not mean that open houses attract only lookers. Quite the contrary, they attract sincere buyers. It's just that they are most frequently not buyers for the house that's open.

Agents hold open houses mainly to find potential clients. Yes, they show the house that's open, but when a buyer doesn't fit, they try to work with that buyer to find a house he or she does want. In other words, for agents open houses are a major source of picking up clients, both buyers and sometimes sellers who have to get rid of their existing house before they can purchase.

You, on the other hand, have only one house to sell. If the people coming through don't want to purchase your home, you can't very well interest them in another property or offer to list their existing homes. Thus, in theory, if the vast majority of people who stop won't want to purchase your house, holding an open house is largely a waste of your time.

I said in theory. In practice remember that your house is open virtually all the time. Any time a buyer wants to see it, all he has to do is call up, give his name, phone number and address and you'll show it to him. So what's an open house for a FSBO seller?

For you, holding an open house means that on a Sunday you will hang a sign in front saying "House Open" and will welcome anyone and everyone who comes by (though not necessarily including the neighborhood kids, dogs and cats). Just as it would if you listed with an agent, your house will be available to be seen by the public.

The trouble, of course, is that statistically almost everyone who stops by will *not* be interested in your house. Then, there's the matter of security. Do you want just anyone tracking into your home?

If you're not bothered by security concerns, you may want to try one open house just to see how it goes. Who knows? You may beat the odds and find a buyer ready, willing and able who will walk into the front door.

On the other hand, the safe way is to forget about open houses. Leave them to agents. My own feeling is that you won't be losing very much.

Calling Back the Prospect

Perhaps the most important call you'll make when selling your property is the *callback*. Some buyers came out, gave you their names, addresses and phone numbers, looked at your house and left. If you don't call them back, you may never see them again. Also, you may lose a deal that could have been made.

I can't think of the number of times I've called back potential buyers only to have them tell me, "Yes, we were thinking about your house, it's really nice, we like it and probably would make an offer on it. But we just never got around to calling you."

Don't wait for buyers to call you. Almost all buyers suffer from a kind of forgetfulness that sets in as soon as they see your property. I suspect that it comes about because they feel if they call you back, you'll think that they surely want it, will pay full price, will give you cash and will meet all your other terms. They may simply be afraid to call you for fear of giving you the wrong impression. (Translate that to mean a strong bargaining position.)

I can recall talking to buyers who were actually mad at agents (in this case) who didn't call them back when they were really interested in the house. "That so-and-so agent dropped me. What kind of irresponsible action is that?"

I sometimes remind such people that a phone line works both ways: If they were really interested, they could call the agent or the seller direct, but, somehow, they just never do.

The point is, don't wait around for potential buyers to call you. After a day or two, call back. It could make you a deal.

What To Say on the Callback

Obviously you will introduce yourself, mention the house they saw and then ask something like, "Did you have any further thoughts on the house?" or, "Was there something more about the house you'd like to see?" (thereby offering to show it again).

If the potential buyer reacts by saying, yes, he or she really did like the house and would like to see it again or, miracle of miracles, "Yes, I'd like to talk about a deal with you," you're on your way.

More than likely, however, the buyer will be restrained, noncommittal and try to get off the phone as quickly as possible. If that's the case, you *probably* have a looker and not a buyer (at least not for your house). However, don't give up. Just because you don't get a "yes" right off the bat doesn't mean that you're getting a "no."

Always Ask, "What's Wrong?"

After a bit of small talk, ask what's wrong with your house. This is not to say that there is anything wrong with the place.

FIGURE 8.5   Common Reasons Given for Not Buying

1. Not the right location

2. Too big/small, not enough bedrooms/too many bedrooms

3. Too expensive/poor terms

4. Poor condition

5. Lacks features (air conditioning, central heating, new carpeting, big yard, etc.)

What you should try to determine, however, is what the buyers see as a problem. In other words, find out the buyers' main objection to your property. You might ask a question such as, "What about the property doesn't appeal to you?" or, "Is there something about the house that you don't like?"

The potential buyers, if they are even remotely interested in the property, should now explain to you why they aren't willing to buy it. The reasons they give could be anything, but Figure 8.5 shows a few of the more common ones.

If you can get a single, good reason that they don't want to buy the house, chances are that you've got real buyers on your hands. Now, all you have to do is turn that negative into a positive and you've got a sale.

Can you do it? Sometimes.

For example, if the problem is price or terms, you can agree to negotiate. This should heat up the buyers' enthusiasm and should result in both of you getting together to discuss things further.

On the other hand, if the house is in the wrong location, there's very little you can say or do. You can point out, for example, "For the location, the price is very good. If you want a better location, you're going to have to pay a whole lot more. Do you have that much more money to spend?"

If the buyers don't have enough money to move to a better location, then you're dealing with the champagne tastes and beer pocketbook mentality. Your job is to convince the buyers of the

FIGURE 8.6 **"Rules for Dealing with Potential Buyers' Objections.**

1. Turn a negative into a positive.
2. Try to get them to come and see the house again.
3. Don't give up.

reality of the real estate market. Ask them if they've looked around at other houses. (You should have already done this yourself when you established the price.) Explain to them that for what they want to spend, they simply won't be able to do better than your house. In short, try to bring them down to reality.

On the other hand, if it turns out that they can spend more money for a better area, you can point out that they can also spend less. Why spend more when they can have all the features of your house for less money?

You won't overcome every potential buyer's objections with this strategy, but it's worth a shot. Be creative. As long as you're on the phone, you've still got a potential deal. My suggestion is that no matter how negative the answers may seem, try to follow the rules for dealing with potential buyers' objections in Figure 8.6.

If the buyers simply aren't interested, don't want to talk anymore and say "Good-bye!" well, it's just one that got away, for today. My suggestion is to put their names on a back page and call again in two or three weeks. Maybe they will have seen more of the market and rethought their priorities.

Yes, you may make a bit of a pest out of yourself. But if you're polite, charming and even, if possible, witty, they'll overlook that. After all, most sales are made simply because the seller is persistent.

Create a Visitor Book

Ask everyone who comes to see your house to sign a visitor book if he or she might even remotely be perceived as a serious

FIGURE 8.7   Visitor Book Information

Name

Address

Phone number

Comments

buyer. If you ask visitors to do this just as they come into the house, most people will be happy to oblige as a courtesy to you.

The visitor book should provide space for the minimal information in Figure 8.7. You can also solicit written comments. Some sellers ask visitors to indicate the kind of property they are looking for (number of bedrooms and bathrooms, location, price, etc.) as a way of determining who is a more likely buyer than another.

There are two purposes for having visitors sign the book. The first is to provide you with a means of contacting them later on. (See the phone callback discussion above.)

The second is to provide the name and address of every buyer who came by in the event that you later on list the property. You can specify in the listing, even in an exclusive-right-to-sell listing, that if anyone to whom you showed the house *before* the listing term buys it, you don't have to pay a commission. Your visitor book is the proof of who was there and who wasn't.

Don't underestimate the value of the visitor book. It can lead you back to a looker who becomes a buyer. It can save you a commission. A FSBO seller who doesn't have a visitor book is overlooking an enormous resource.

Note: Any book or even a sheet of paper will do. However, if you go to the stationery store, you can pick up ready-made visitor books. Usually they are designed for receptions or weddings, but they can easily fill the need here. Just be sure that *at the top of each page*, you clearly print (or type) the information you want visitors to record (see Figure 8.8).

FIGURE 8.8

 Typical Visitor Book

Our Address: 2341 Maple St.
Our Phone: 555-4352

Thanks for looking at our For Sale By Owner home. So that we have a record of those people who stop by, please list the following information:

Name _____
Phone Number _____
Address _____
City, State, ZIP _____
Comments _____

Name _____
Phone Number _____
Address _____
City, State, ZIP _____
Comments _____

Name _____
Phone Number _____
Address _____
City, State, ZIP _____
Comments _____

Name _____
Phone Number _____
Address _____
City, State, ZIP _____
Comments _____

When You Get a Real Live Buyer

One of these days, perhaps sooner than you imagined, you will find a buyer who says, "Yes, I want to purchase your home." You will haggle over the price, the terms, perhaps even the light fixture in the dining room, but ultimately, the buyer will want to purchase and you'll sag back with a sigh of relief telling yourself, "At last, it's over!"

Be forewarned. "It ain't over yet!"

Between the time a buyer agrees to purchase and the time that title transfers and you receive your money is a long and arduous process with many hoops to get through. In Chapter 10, we'll cover the steps you'll want to take, but an early word of caution: qualify your buyer.

Qualification: The Key to a Successful Sale

Your best hope of successfully completing the sale is qualifying your buyer up front. As soon as a buyer indicates a willingness to purchase, it's your turn to ask questions. As noted in earlier chapters, find out just how much the buyer's income really is. If it isn't quite enough, ask yourself if you really want to continue with the deal.

Once the buyer commits to buy, ask point-blank about credit. Are there any little blemishes here or there? A history of late payments can disqualify a buyer from getting a mortgage in today's strict lending market.

Find out exactly how much cash the buyer has and be sure it's enough for the down payment and closing costs. Remember, the lender will want to see exactly where the buyer is getting the down payment (to be sure it's not borrowed).

Once you've got a buyer who agrees to purchase, don't be squeamish about asking these questions. It may turn out that you won't want to sell to this buyer because he or she really isn't qualified and signing a sales agreement would only mean tying up your, home unnecessarily.

CHAPTER

NINE

How To Prepare Your House for Showing

If there's anything I've learned in my years in real estate, it's that buyers have no imagination.

I mean that buyers almost universally only see what's in front of them. They believe, almost absolutely, only what they can see.

For example, your home may boast an absolutely smashing entry with tile floors, wood trim, solid oak doors, marble columns and more, but, if the floor, walls and doors have been painted over with a dull ugly paint, that's what the buyer will see—the dull paint, not the quality beneath.

Nevermind explaining about the oak wood and tile and marble underneath. Ninety-nine percent of buyers won't pay any attention to it. All they'll see and remember is an ugly painted entry, and they'll probably dismiss your home from their minds as a contender for purchase.

Even worse, let's say that you've got a wonderful home inside. Everything is neat, clean, well kept and looks good, but you didn't get around to taking good care of your lawn this year and the shrubs out front are wild because they weren't trimmed, and the paint has weathered and has peeling patches. Many buyers won't even bother to stop and look inside! Nevermind that the inside of your home is beautiful. The outside will chill them and they'll drive on, never knowing what they missed.

As I said, the rule is:

 Rule for Showing Your House

Buyers believe what they see—they have no imagination.

That's what you have to work with. That's where you must begin when you prepare your house for showing. Therefore, your first job is to bypass the buyers' imagination and give them something straightforward and direct to look at. You must make your house appear smashing, wonderful, exciting, glamorous, even sexy, for that first impression. Don't let those buyers wonder about your place. Tell it all at a glance. Make your house look so splendid that even someone with 20/100 vision will turn around to admire it. In other words, leave *nothing* to the buyers' imagination, because they don't have any.

What To Do First

Once you decide on the need to spruce up the place a bit to catch prospective buyers' attention, most sellers are immediately stopped by economic considerations. (By the way, sprucing up is really a minimum—you need to set a fire under buyers to get them to move, but it's a starting place for us here.) Few sellers have a lot of money to spend. Short of taking out a home equity loan, you probably can't afford to fix up the old house the way it should look. Yes, you want to sell, but you don't want to bankrupt yourself doing it. Yes, you agree that you need to prepare the home for showing, but you can't afford, don't have the time or lack the energy to do it all.

What can and should you do first?

 Rule for Preparing Your House

First do everything that's inexpensive.

Concentrate on What Costs Little

This can be a tough concept for some people. The truth is that which makes the biggest impression often costs the least to do.

Let's take a few examples:

You decide to redo your family room. It's going to cost $3,000 for a wall of new bookshelves, $1,500 for new carpeting and $500 for great new window coverings. In short, you're looking at an expenditure of about $5,000.

But, you say to yourself, think of what I'll get when I sell. Right?

Wrong. Chances are that your work in the family room, admirable though it may be, won't get you a quicker sale or a higher price. In short, while you'll be spending time, money and effort, you'll be getting nothing in return except satisfaction. (Remember your goal: You're not after satisfaction—you're after a sale!)

When a buyer comes in and "oohs and ahhs" about your family room, that person is really saying silently, "What an idiot that seller is to waste all that money on the family room. Of course, if I buy I'll enjoy it, but why should I pay a dime more for it?"

Or another example:

Your backyard looks like a toxic dump site. So, you haul in sand and topsoil, build a deck and overhang, plant shrubs and flowers, and put in a small pond with a couple of fish. In short, you transform that toxic dump site into scenic park land.

Now, any buyer's going to be knocked over backward upon seeing your yard and rush to buy the property, right?

Wrong!

Ninety-nine percent of buyers love a great backyard, but won't pay ten cents more for it. It won't compel them to buy any quicker, either. They'll look at the front yard and the house and the first impression it gave, and if that's good, then they'll think about the backyard and add it in as a free plus.

In short, all that time, money and effort spent on the backyard gets you a passing nod, but it doesn't make your house that much more salable.

I realize that this may fly in the face of what you have been told about selling, but I believe it to be the real truth. What gets a buyer's attention is that first impression and what makes a good first impression does not cost much. Indeed, good first impressions are often made by simple cosmetic changes.

Think of the old Hollywood sets. Remember, they used to have entire cities that were nothing more than breakfronts. They consisted of the front of a building held up with posts with no sides, back or top, but when we watched the movie, the place looked authentic; it looked convincing; it made a strong, believable impression on us.

The same holds true for your house. The truth is that what you need to do is the cosmetic work. It's not expensive and it will make a big difference in terms of getting you a quicker sale and a better price.

The Under-$500 Fix-Up

If you want to know what to do to effectively prepare your house for sale, Figure 9.1 gives you a short shopping list.

FIGURE 9.1   The Under-$500 House Preparation

1. Mow the front lawn, water it, fertilize it and get it to look great. Cost: $50

2. Plant new shrubs in front and trim old ones. Plant colorful flowers near the entrance. Clean the driveway and any cement paths. If the entrance walk is broken or damaged, pull it out and replace it with inexpensive stepping stones. Make the front look terrific. Cost: $250 to $300

3. Paint the front of your house. Use a good paint and a separate trim paint. Do an especially good job on the front door. Use a neutral color. Cost for paint: $50

4. Paint the inside entry of your home as well as the living room, dining room and kitchen. Use a neutral color. Cost for paint: $50

5. Take half the furniture in your house and store it someplace else, preferably off the property. Put it in a relative's or a neighbor's garage. Cost: 0

Total cost:

Front cleanup	$ 50
Entry fix-up	250
Front painting	50
Inside painting	50
Furniture removal	0
Total	$400

In short, for under $500 you can dramatically improve any buyer's first impression of your property. By so doing you will automatically increase your chances of a quicker sale and a higher price.

Remember, don't rely on the buyer's imagination. You have to transform what the buyer first sees from something that's poor or mediocre to something that looks great. When that buyer walks in, he or she won't have to imagine what your house could look like if this were mowed, or that were trimmed, or the other were painted. It will be spelled out for them—no imagination required. Instead of a hard-to-read book, you'll give the buyer an easy-to-view movie. Instead of what could be, you'll be showing what is. Instead of maybe, your buyer will be thinking, "yes!"

Before moving on, a word about moving half the furniture out. You may be wondering what that's about. The truth is that buyers want spacious houses. Yet most of us make our houses look small by cluttering them with too much furniture. Of course, there are exceptions. If you've had an interior designer create your home's interior with matched furniture, carpeting, wall and window coverings and so forth, you probably won't want to remove anything.

On the other hand, if the interior design of your home was directed, like mine, by what's in your pocketbook, you bought what furniture you could find when it was on sale. That means that your house has an eclectic style, a little of this, a little of that. You bought what you wanted, what you liked, what felt comfortable to you, what was affordable. As a result, total strangers with totally different likes and dislikes who walk through will probably think that the place looks more like a den (as in animal) than a presentation. They will undoubtedly wonder at your taste, which simply means it's different from their own. Most of all, instead of remembering how spacious your place is, they'll recall it as a jumble of crowded, uncoordinated furniture.

How do you avoid this? Remove half your furniture. When the place looks too empty to you, too thinned out, too foreign, it will probably look great to buyers. Remember, buyers are visualizing how their furniture will look in your home. It's important to give them the impression that their furniture will fit.

Working with the Time-Line Concept

I am not suggesting that you do only inexpensive, cosmetic things but that you do those inexpensive projects *first*. As time passes and no buyer materializes, you may want to move forward with more expensive, material improvements. Again, these should be eye-catching first, but they should be undertaken only after you've first done the inexpensive, cosmetic stuff.

Let's take a look at another example:

Helen and Peter have owned their home for seven years. They've decided to sell FSBO. Now they're preparing the property. When they first put the house up for sale, they cleaned and trimmed the front yard and painted the outside front as well as the entry and big rooms inside. In short, they did all the cosmetic, inexpensive things.

It's been a couple of months now, and although they've had some nibbles, there hasn't been a buyer ready, willing and able to purchase the property. The housing market isn't good in their area and there are few buyers. Helen and Peter are beginning to think that they need to do more to improve the appearance of their property. What should they do next?

My suggestion to them, and to you, is to do those things that are going to make the biggest impact on buyers, yet cost the least amount of money. Let's begin at the beginning, the front door. (Note: The following suggestions are in the order that they should be performed. I would do the first one first. Then the next, and so on. Ideally, you will have sold the house long before you get to the more expensive items at the end of the list.)

The Front Door

The first thing that anyone sees about your house, at least the interior of it, is the front door. Thus, the quality of your front door makes the first, lasting impression.

For this reason, I suggested earlier that you give the front door a good coat of paint when you were fixing up the front of your house. Now, if you intend to do more, I suggest you start here and replace the door(s).

A new front door isn't that expensive at discount lumber stores. You can get a good one in solid birch or mahogany for around $150. For another $100 you can get it in oak. Add in the costs of stain, the hardware and installation and you can have a brand new front door for around $300 to $500.

Seem like a lot of money? It's not when you think of the impression it makes. A great-looking front door will knock the socks off potential buyers. I believe it returns far more than it costs in your ability to resell quicker and at a higher price.

Painting

After you've painted the front of the house and the entry rooms and fixed up the front door, I suggest that you continue to paint the rest of the house. The next rooms to paint would be the kitchen, the guest bathroom and the master bedroom, then all the other rooms.

Paint them from floor to ceiling and choose a neutral color. It's important that the color be a beige, white or light color of some sort because many people are offended by stronger colors. I'd avoid blues, greens and yellows. Yes, you may find a buyer who loves a specific color. But for each one of that kind of buyer, you'll come across 50 others who hate it. You have to play the odds and go with the most neutral colors.

By the way, if your house has an acoustical ceiling, popular in some parts of the country for the past couple of decades, and it's dirty, what do you do? Do you paint it?

You can. Except that it soaks up paint. It could cost you as much in time and money to paint an acoustical ceiling as it would to paint the entire rest of the inside as well as the outside of the house.

My suggestion is that you hire an acoustical contractor to reblow the ceilings. It isn't that expensive, often under $1,000 for an entire typical medium-sized house. And the difference it makes is striking. It will refresh your house and help make it look new again.

Carpeting

Thus far we've discussed items that are relatively inexpensive to do. Now we come to a big, expensive item, yet one that makes an enormous impression on buyers.

When you first walk into a house or an office or any new building, your eyes tend to drift down. We all tend to look at the floor. What do we see? Is your flooring bright, clean and new looking? Or, is it dirty, worn and frayed?

If it's the latter, it will make a big difference in a buyer's mind. Never mind pointing out that the buyer can replace the carpeting. You have to show buyers what the house will look like with new carpeting, not just ask them to imagine it.

My suggestion is that if you're pressed for money, at the least call in a professional carpet and floor cleaning service and have them do your house. *Don't try to save money and do it yourself.*

Professional services can make even an old, worn-out carpet look better. They can make a floor shine. And in most cases they can do it for a couple of hundred dollars. The steam ejector that you rent from the local supermarket may only pump dirt from one part of the carpet to another.

On the other hand, if you're really serious about selling and you have the money (or can take out a home equity loan), the best bet is to put brand-new carpeting in the home. Brand-new, inexpensive carpeting looks almost as good as brand-new, expensive carpeting, and it looks a whole lot better than old carpeting, even some that's been cleaned.

How much does new carpeting cost? Be aware that it's probably a lot cheaper than you think. If you walk into big-name department stores or even major carpeting stores, you're quite likely to spend perhaps $20 to $30 a yard. There's nine square feet in a square yard, so if your home has 1,500 square feet of space that needs carpeting, you're talking about 167 yards, which works out to around $3,500 at $20 a yard (including taxes) to over $5,000 at $30 a yard. Either way, it's big bucks.

Only you needn't spend that much. Check with some real estate professionals in your area, particularly those who handle residential property management. They are always replacing carpeting in homes. Typically they use a carpet broker.

A carpet broker buys directly from the mill and then sells directly to you. Often he or she does not have a store, but instead comes to your home to show you a limited number of samples.

Don't be put off by the small selection. Remember, you're not installing carpeting to walk on. You're putting in carpeting that will sell your house. All that you need is a neutral color (that will appeal to most people) and a good-looking weave.

The price? I have put brokered carpeting in houses I was preparing to sell that cost from $9 to $15 a yard installed. It compared favorably with carpeting costing twice that price available through retail outlets. In short, you can save half the cost. For a 1,500-square-foot house, it might cost you only between $1,500 and $2,000 to install a good grade of quite nice-looking carpeting.

A quick additional word about color. The rule is that the carpeting always tends to look lighter when installed than it does when you look at a sample. When you're buying to live in the house, therefore, most people select darker carpeting. It doesn't show the dirt as much and it requires less cleaning.

On the other hand, when you're installing carpet to sell, the rule is *buy lighter carpeting.* I have installed nearly white carpeting in homes I was preparing to sell. I wouldn't think of living in the house myself because I'd have to take off my shoes before walking on it for fear of tracking in dirt that would show.

As a presentation, however, it makes the house look fabulous. Here's a case where you can take advantage of the buyer's lack of imagination. Buyers see the light carpeting and think how wonderful it looks, while not imagining all the problems it will cause when they have to live with it.

Rehabbing/Renovating

Finally, there's the matter of spending even bigger bucks to renovate a kitchen or a bath, enlarge or add on a room and do other similar work. Does this ever pay off?

Sometimes, but not often. Here's an example:

Jan and Jim felt that their old-fashioned kitchen detracted from their house. So they looked into replacing the cabinets and found it would cost around $3,000; a new countertop and other costs ran the total up to about $5,000. It would cost them about $5,000 to rehabilitate their kitchen.

On the other hand, there was an alternative. Jim filled in the cracks and holes in the cabinets' surfaces, rehung the doors and then painted them all. They had been a natural stained wood. But they were old, scuffed and worn. Now they offered a bright, clean, painted look that was very modern. In addition, he repainted the rest of the kitchen and put in new light fixtures, an inexpensive new countertop plus a sink and new faucets. The total cost was under $500.

Did it look as good as a totally rehabilitated kitchen? No. Did it look good enough to sell the house? Certainly.

Remember, *your goal is to sell the property, not to spend money.*

The same holds true for bathrooms and other rooms. When you're going to sell, spend the lowest amount that will give you a good-looking result. Often, cleaning, painting and touching up can make whatever you're working on look quite appealing at a tenth of the cost of replacing.

For a more detailed explanation of what and how to renovate inexpensively and successfully, I suggest that you check into my book, *The Home Remodeling Organizer* (Chicago: Dearborn Financial Publishing, Inc., 1995).

One last word on additions and enlargements. Don't do them, unless a house simply won't sell because it lacks something that people want. Maybe the kitchen is just too small. Or maybe there's no family room. Or maybe there's no fireplace.

Whatever the cause, to sell quicker and for a better price, you may have to add or enlarge. If that's the case, I suggest you either lower your price to the point where people will buy the property in spite of the defect, or bite the bullet and do the work.

Keep in mind, however, that adding or enlarging is the costliest of all enterprises. It takes dollars, time and great effort.

The Backyard

As noted earlier, I don't think much of spending money on the backyard. My feeling is that the vast majority of buyers are not swayed one way or another by a backyard. Therefore, this is the last place I would spend money.

Yes, I would pay the kid down the street $20 to mow the weeds down, but no, I wouldn't spend a dime more than that.

You may be asking, what about all the attributes of a back-yard such as a sun deck, overhang to offer shade, spa, pool, flower garden and other amenities?

All of these are often more of a headache than they are worth. Let's take a swimming pool as an example. Today, to put in a decent-sized swimming pool with adequate decking and equipment could easily cost $25,000, but when it comes time to sell, can you get an additional $25,000 for the property?

Quite the contrary. Many buyers specify that the house they buy must *not* have a pool. They don't want the hassle of cleaning it and keeping up the chemicals. In short, you may lose as many buyers as you get by trying to sell a house with a pool.

But, what about price? Won't buyers pay more for a pool house than for one without?

Marginally, yes. In parts of California, pool homes tend to sell for perhaps $5,000 more, on average, when they sell, than houses without pools, but that's a far cry from the $25,000 it costs to put in that pool.

If you have a house with a pool, make the best of it. Keep the pool spotless and well chlorinated—and hope that you find a buyer who's willing to pay extra to have it.

If you don't already have a pool, bite your tongue every time you want to mention the idea of adding one. I've owned many properties with pools and still own several today, and I can assure you that I have never received any financial benefit from them. In fact, they have always been more of a headache than they are worth.

Also, keep in mind your house's location when deciding what home improvements and upgrades to make. If you have the only house in the neighborhood with an in-ground pool, it will be tougher to get more money for the house.

The same holds true, to a lesser degree, for just about any other feature in the backyard. If you already have a spa, deck, gardens, overhang and so on in your backyard, they will undoubt-edly be additional selling pluses for the house, although I doubt that they will get you an additional dollar in price. On the other hand, if you don't have them, you would be just throwing money away to put them in.

Home Fix-Up For-Sale Checklist

We've looked at the different things you can do to prepare your home for sale. You'll find other suggestions in Chapter 7, such as getting the right kind of sign to put in front, but for here, let's recap and check off those that are aimed at making the property look more salable. Figure 9.2 is an improvement/fix-up checklist. It's also put together in the form of that timeline. Do the least expensive, most impressive things first. Save those big-ticket, less-noticeable items for the very last.

How To Deal With Major Expense Items That Don't Show

Finally, we come to those items that cost a fortune to fix or replace, yet don't make any difference when it comes to appearance. I'm speaking of such things as the heating/air-conditioning system, the electrical/plumbing system, the roof (although depending on the type, some roofs will look bad when they get old and deteriorate), and broken foundations among others.

Often fixing, replacing or adding these items can cost many thousands of dollars, yet doing so won't significantly alter the presentation of the property.

Should you spend the money?

My feeling is that you shouldn't. As we'll see in Chapter 12, you should definitely tell the buyer of any problems. However, you should then negotiate the cost of getting the problem fixed, replaced or added.

For example, I recently sold a home that had no air-conditioning, yet it was located in a moderately warm area. The buyer wanted air-conditioning for the summer months.

I explained that the house had been built without air and previous owners hadn't minded it. The buyer wasn't satisfied, so I

FIGURE 9.2

☑ **House Fix-Up Checklist**

LEAST EXPENSIVE/MUST DO

1. Mow the lawn and keep it mowed. _____
2. Replant grass in bare spots and fertilize lawn. _____
3. Trim all the hedges. _____
4. Plant hedges in bare spots. _____
5. Clean off driveway/remove oil stains. _____
6. Clean/fix front walkways. _____
7. Paint front of house. _____
8. Paint front doors. _____
9. Replace broken screens/windows in front. _____
10. Paint entry rooms (such an entry, living room, family room, etc.). _____
11. Remove half the furniture in the house. (Don't store it in the garage; leave it at a relative's or neighbor's home, or put it in a rental space area.) _____

MORE EXPENSIVE/OPTIONAL FIX-UP WORK

12. Replace the front door(s). _____
13. Paint the entire inside of the house. _____
14. Reblow acoustical ceilings. _____
15. Clean or, if possible, replace all carpeting throughout house. Clean or, if possible, refinish all bare flooring. _____
16. Repaint or restain cabinets in the kitchen. _____
17. Replace light fixtures. _____

FIGURE 9.2 *(Continued)*

18. Repaint or restain cabinets in bathrooms.   _____

19. Add on or enlarge as a last resort.   _____

20. Paint sides and rear outside of house.   _____

THINGS NOT TO DO

1. Don't add a pool, spa, deck, lawn or shrubs to the   _____
   backyard.

2. Don't enlarge or add on unless it's to correct a   _____
   defect in the house.

3. Don't spend money on major fix-up jobs that   _____
   don't show such as replacing a roof or heating
   system.

dropped the price an additional $1,000. Now, the buyer was happy.

Should you go forward and spend the money?

The point here is that almost always, big-ticket items are negotiable. New air-conditioning probably would have cost me $2,000, but here I negotiated a reduction for half what it would have cost me and made the buyer quite happy.

In another case, a house I was selling had a wood shingle roof that had deteriorated. It was leaking and old and needed to be replaced. A whole new roof would have cost around $10,000, but to fix just the areas that were bad with a guarantee of no leaks for a year would only have cost around $2,500.

The buyer ultimately wanted a complete new roof and wouldn't be satisfied with less. However, I explained that I was willing to spend only the $2,500 in repair work. We compromised: in that I gave him the $2,500, which he then applied toward the $10,000 replacement job after the sale. On the other hand, if I had gone ahead with the repair work, the buyer still wouldn't have been satisfied (since he wanted nothing less than a new roof) and I would still have had to negotiate a price concession. Not doing the work actually paid off.

In most cases, it pays not to do big-ticket items, but instead to point them out to the buyer and then negotiate an amount acceptable to all, which can be in the form of a sales price reduction. More often than not, this will be more acceptable to the buyer and will get you a quicker and even higher-priced sale.

CHAPTER
TEN

Helping Buyers Get a Mortgage

It would really be nice if a buyer came in and offered to pay for your home in cash, but, don't expect it to happen any time soon. Almost all residential real estate is financed—your buyer will need a mortgage.

What's more, if you want a sale, it's probably up to you to help the buyer get that financing. However, I've heard many a seller say, "Why should I help the buyer with the financing? After all, isn't it up to the buyer to arrange for that? Isn't it up to the buyer to come up with the purchase money?"

Of course it is. Of course it's the buyer's responsibility to arrange for financing. However, most buyers are lost when it comes to arranging the financing. They simply don't have a clue as to how to go about doing it.

In a sale involving an agent, that agent will usually explain to the buyers where to get financing and what kinds of mortgages are available. The agent will qualify the buyer and determine how much the buyer can really afford to pay. Then, the agent will steer that buyer toward a suitable lender.

When you sell FSBO, you can do no less. If the buyer knows nothing about financing, you need to step in and provide the information. If you don't do as much, you could lose a sale.

In this chapter we're going to examine just what you need to do to help the buyer with financing. No, you needn't become an expert in mortgages to sell by FSBO, but you do have to do your homework and learn the basics so that you can at least qualify a potential buyer and point out the various loans available to him or her on your property.

Qualifying the Buyer

A good rule of thumb is that only one out of every three people who look at your house can really afford to buy it. If your house is priced below $100,000, then a larger percentage of the buyers will probably qualify for the needed mortgage. If it's over $100,000, then probably a lower percentage will qualify.

What this means is that when you eventually get someone who says he or she is ready and willing to purchase, first you have to determine if the party is able to do so. It may turn out that the thrill of getting a buyer will fade when you discover that he or she has bad credit, doesn't have enough income or hasn't got a big enough bank account to make the purchase.

While the lender will make the final determination of who can and who can't qualify for a mortgage, you should at least do the preliminary work yourself. Before proceeding to the sales agreement with the attorney or agent, as described in Chapter 6, you should get some important answers about your buyer's ability to qualify.

How To Handle the Touchy Subject of Credit and Income

Because you are the seller, many buyers will hesitate to reveal necessary financial information to you. They may fear that you will use it to gain leverage in negotiating the price. Or they may simply feel that it's none of your business.

On the other hand, you will need to know some information about their credit history, their income and their available cash in order to determine whether they will qualify to purchase your home.

The real trick is to get the information without scaring the buyers away. My suggestion is that you *don't* simply come out and ask such direct questions as, "How much money do you make?" or, "Do you have any bad credit?" At least, don't ask them at the beginning of negotiations. The buyers may simply decide that you're too nosy and may take their business elsewhere.

On the other hand, I suggest that you *do* drop hints early on about what it takes to buy your home. For example, as the buyers begin to show significant interest, you can explain that if they plan to put the standard 20 percent down, their payments at then-current interest rates will likely be around $X per month.

You can watch their reactions. Do they seem to feel that's acceptable? Or do they blink, look astonished and give the impression that it's an impossibly high figure? If it's the latter, I wouldn't start sending out change of address notices quite yet.

Similarly, you may note that in today's mortgage market, it's difficult to get good financing with any credit blemishes at all. You might say something such as, "I don't suppose you have any concerns there, do you?"

Again, watch the reaction. Many times buyers with bad credit will deny it or will hem and haw. However, buyers with good credit very often simply will say, "We have excellent credit and have no problems there." If your buyers don't come out and tell you they have good credit, be suspicious.

Wait until They Are Committed

Beyond following the suggestions provided above, I caution that you not go any further in qualifying your buyers until they are committed. By committed, I mean that you and they have gone through the worksheet agreement in Chapter 6 and reached a consensus on terms and price.

You may, however, be asked by the buyers at any stage along the way about the kind of financing that's available on the property. You should have done your homework and be ready to pop up with the appropriate answers. We'll have more to say about this later in this chapter.

Once They Are Committed

Once your buyers have filled out the worksheet and you've agreed on price and terms, then you should at least determine whether they have a chance of getting financing on the property. This is important to you because, if they can't get financing and you go forward with the sale, you'd be taking your house off the market and tying it up perhaps for months before finding out they really couldn't buy.

I suggest that you explain the situation to the buyers in exactly those terms. They now want to buy and are probably eager to do so. You've agreed on a price. However, before you agree to sell and take your house off the market, you need to know something about them: that they will qualify for the mortgage. They should understand that they now have to divulge some information to convince you to sell. You can tell them about the two ways of handling this.

Having the Buyers Go to a Lender

If you're dealing with touchy buyers, those who really don't feel comfortable letting you know their financing, the easiest strategy is to give them the names of one or two mortgage brokers (discussed shortly). Tell them that you'll give them seven days in which to get a letter of preliminary loan approval.

This means that they have seven days to go to the mortgage broker and fill out the mortgage application. The broker then must secure a credit report and, if they qualify, issue you a letter of preliminary qualification.

Sound simple?

The problem is that you'll be taking your house off the market during that period of time. Further, to be sure that you have a deal, you'll want a sales agreement that is filled out and signed. Thus, you'll have the expense of the lawyer or the agent's time in that regard. While this may be an easy way to go, it can also be an expensive one, particularly if it turns out that the buyers don't qualify! You could end up spending the money and having nothing to show for it. This exercise will get stale very quickly after you go through it a couple of times.

Qualifying the Buyers Yourself

The other way to go is to insert a step before the previous one. In other words, before filling out the documents and having the buyers get the preliminary qualification letter, you can qualify the buyers yourself.

As noted, the problem here is that touchy buyers might balk at giving you personal financial information. That's the risk. The reward is that if you get it, you get a better idea if the buyers will qualify before spending any money on an agent or attorney.

You can use the fill-in chart in Figure 10.1 to qualify the buyer. It asks only a minimum of information, yet will at least give you a good idea of whether your buyer can qualify for the mortgage necessary to purchase your property.

How To Use the "Buyer Qualification Chart"

If the buyers fill out the buyer qualification chart even partially, you may get enough information to determine quickly if they qualify for the payments on your property. Keep in mind, however, that you can only request this information—you can't demand it. If the buyers refuse, then you can either not sell the

FIGURE 10.1

Buyer Qualification Chart

(All information voluntarily submitted)

Name _____

Address _____

Phone Number _____

Income _____

What is your monthly gross income?

Husband $_____

Wife $_____

Other source $_____

                          Total $_____

What are the monthly payments on your long-term debt including:

Car payments $_____

Credit cards $_____

Alimony $_____

Loans $_____

Other $_____

                     Less Total $_____

            Total Income Available $_____

Credit History

Do you have any foreclosures?	Yes _____	No _____
Did you file bankruptcy in the past 10 years?	Yes _____	No _____
Did you have any delinquent loans in the past 7 years?	Yes _____	No _____
Did you have any late payments (where you paid a penalty) in the past 5 years?	Yes _____	No _____
Do you know of any credit problems you may have?	Yes _____	No _____

FIGURE 10.1 *(Continued)*

Cash To Make Down Payment
 The cash required to purchase this home including
 closing costs is $ _____
 Do you have this money in checking/savings?   Yes ____ No ____
 Do you have it in another source such as a CD?   Yes ____ No ____
 Are you borrowing it from relatives?   Yes ____ No ____
 Will they cosign the loan?   Yes ____ No ____
 Are you borrowing it from a bank or other lender? Yes ____ No ____

property to them or go ahead with the first plan, create and sign the documents and give them a week to get preliminary approval from a lender. Note that a lender's preliminary letter is *not* binding; it's to help you find out whether you have a qualified buyer.

Monthly Gross Income

Most buyers won't hesitate to tell you their monthly gross income. They usually understand that income is critical to buying a property, and they will want to let you know that they make enough to qualify.

What you need to know is that in order to get most new first mortgages for 80 percent of the sales price, the total payment cannot be more than around a third of the buyers' gross income (before taxes).

See Figure 10.2 for an example of the items that go into the *monthly* payment calculation.

In the example, all of the payments come to $1,348. That amount can't be more than about a third of the buyer's income. Simply multiply by three and you get $4,044. That's the minimum total amount of monthly income that the buyers need. If their income is more than that, they probably will qualify. If it's less, they may not. (Actually, this is a very *rough* calculation. Lenders use *front-end* and *back-end* calculations that are far more

FIGURE 10.2   Example of Items That Go into the Monthly Payment Calculation

Principal payment	$ 28
Interest payment	1,000
Tax payment	250
Insurance payment	30
Homeowner's association payment	25
Assessments paid monthly	15
	$1,348

complex. But this will give you a rough idea of the income needed to qualify. If the buyers are very close, they may or may not make it.)

Subtractions from the Buyers' Income

If your buyers indicate sufficient income, don't rejoice quite yet. Keep in mind that from their total income, lenders subtract any long-term payments (typically those lasting four months or longer) that the borrowers may have. These include payments for cars, credit cards, alimony and loans (see Figure 10.3).

Remember that in our example earlier, the buyers had to be making $4,044 to qualify? Well, if they have long-term payments, as in our example, they must have additional income to cover them. In this case you would add the $1,100 to $4,044 and come up with $5,144. To qualify to buy your house, given the long-term payments the buyers have, they would now need to be making $5,144 a month or roughly $60,000 a year. If they aren't, they might not be able to get a new first mortgage.

Buyers Who Don't Want To Tell You Their Long-Term Expenses

One problem you can encounter is buyers who don't want to get into the details with you about their long-term expenses. They

FIGURE 10.3   Buyers' Long-Term Payments To Be Subtracted from Income

Car payments	$ 400
Credit cards	100
Alimony	400
Loans	150
Other	50
Total	$1,100

don't want to tell you about alimony or car payments. They may figure it's none of your business.

If that's the case, then ask them to forget about listing the individual long-term expenses. Just ask them for a total. "What is your total monthly payment for loans or whatever that run more than four months?" They are much more likely to give you this figure. (The specifics, after all, are more to remind them what to include than to give you needed information. To make your calculation, you need only the total.)

Note: Buyers can reduce their long-term monthly expenses by paying off some debt, such as credit card balances. This will help them improve their income ratios.

Credit History

You might think that the information here is so personal that most buyers would not want to disclose it, but my experience is that they often don't mind. Those who have no problems disclosing information usually are proud to give it to you. Those who do have problems want to get them into the open so that the problems can be dealt with and overcome. If you're concerned that your buyers may be hiding some information, you can point out that every lender will run a simple credit check, which should reveal all of this information anyway.

Foreclosures

Answering "yes" to any or all of the questions doesn't automatically disqualify a buyer from getting a loan. Most lenders will accept letters of explanation, accompanied by documentation, to show that they really weren't at fault. For example, a foreclosure may show up that was really for someone else with a similar name. In my own case a foreclosed mortgage showed up for a property I had sold five years earlier. I simply presented my settlement papers for the deal, which showed that the buyer had assumed the mortgage when I sold the property, and the troubles went away.

However, if your buyers answer "yes" to the first two questions (foreclosure and bankruptcy) without having a good explanation, you could be in trouble. Many lenders simply won't consider them.

Delinquencies

Delinquent loans and late payments are also undesirable but less condemning, if a good explanation is provided. For example, a bout of illness five years ago could account for late payments or delinquencies on a number of loans. However, if the borrower got well, made them all good and has been current ever since, it's unlikely a lender would deny a mortgage because of the problem.

What should you do if your buyers reveal a serious credit problem? My suggestion is that you state your doubts about their ability to qualify, but since you aren't a lender, you really can't know. Have them see a lender (savings and loan, bank, mortgage broker, etc.) and fill out an application along with a credit report. Ask for the preliminary qualification letter within seven days. I would not, however, take my house off the market, nor would I sign a deal with these buyers until I get that letter.

Yes, I stand a better chance of losing them this way, but I also avoid spending money and tying myself down to a deal with a poor risk.

Getting a Cash Down Payment

The final questions are designed to reveal the source of the buyers' down payment. You don't really care where they're getting it, as long as it isn't borrowed. The rule is that borrowed money cannot be used as a down payment for the purchase of a home when securing a new institutional first mortgage.

If the money is in the bank or a CD, you're home free. If it's from relatives, the lender may balk or may require the relatives to be on the note. It's a maybe sort of problem.

If the money is to be borrowed, you probably have a problem. Again, check into the suggestion at the end of the previous section.

This should give you a good idea of how to qualify your buyer. Using the worksheet and the explanations, you can almost become your own mortgage examiner!

What Kind of Financing Your Buyer Needs

Thus far we've looked at how to qualify your buyers. Now, let's consider the various options that you may be able to offer in terms of purchasing your home. In reality there are only two major ways to purchase (besides paying cash, which you needn't worry about unless you're very lucky): *cash-to-loan* and *seller-assisted financing*. We'll consider each type separately.

Cash-to-Loan

Essentially this means that the buyer gets a new first mortgage from an institution such as a savings and loan association or a bank for a portion of the purchase price, typically 80 or 90 percent, and then pays cash for the balance of 20 or 10 percent. This is the ideal way to sell your home because you get all cash. (That's assuming, of course, that you want all cash. Some sellers prefer to get a portion of the sales price in the form of a mortgage. We'll cover that in the next section.)

FIGURE 10.4   Degree of Difficulty in Getting Financing at Different LTVs

Cash Down	LTV	Difficulty
5%	95%	Very hard to get
10%	90%	More difficult
20%	80%	Most common
40%	60%	No qualifying, but higher interest rate and points

There are a number of tricky things here that you need to be aware of and to watch out for. The first has to do with the loan-to-value ratio or LTV.

The LTV means that amount of the purchase price that is financed through a lender. For example, if the buyer gets financing for 80 percent of the purchase price, the LTV is 80 percent.

What's important to understand is that the lower the LTV, the easier (and usually cheaper in terms of points and other costs) it is to get financing. Thus, a buyer who is able to put 20 percent down to an 80 percent LTV is more likely to qualify than the same buyer who puts down 10 percent and tries to get a 90 percent LTV. The more cash the buyer can come up with, and as a consequence the lower the LTV, the better for you. You may want to consider the chart in Figure 10.4, which lists different LTVs and the difficulties in securing financing for them. (Note: LTV is based on the appraised value of your home. If you've done your homework on pricing [see Chapter 5] you shouldn't have a problem. On the other hand, if the appraiser says your property isn't worth what you're selling it for, either you have to lower your price or the buyer has to come up with more money, a very difficult call to make.)

In this situation, we're assuming a *conventional* loan, which means that there is no government insurance, as in the case of FHA loans, or no guarantee, as in the case of VA loans. FHA loans are more difficult to qualify for. VA loans are less difficult to get, but the buyer must be a veteran having served between certain dates to qualify; check with the Department of Veterans Affairs. In the case of both FHA and VA loans, the property also must qualify; it must pass muster by a special inspection from a government-approved appraiser.

For all conventional loans above 80 percent LTV, the borrower must pay an additional ¼ to ½ percent premium for private mortgage insurance that protects the lender against default.

From your perspective as a seller, if you're looking at cash-to-loan, the more cash the buyers put down, the easier it will be for them to get financing. If I had a choice between a buyer putting 5 percent down and one putting 20 percent down, all else being equal, I'd grab the 20 percent downer.

Seller-Assisted Financing

In a perfect world, all buyers would put at least 20 percent cash down and secure an institutional loan for the balance. In the real world, few buyers have enough cash for the down payment. Thus, buyers may ask you to assist them in making the purchase.

Should you assist with seller financing?

The answer often comes down to something as simple as this: to make the sale, you may have to help with the financing.

You may find that you get lots of lookers trafficking through your property. Some are real buyers who would like to purchase, but no one seems to have the requisite cash down payment. After all, if you're selling your property for $100,000, buyers must come up with $20,000 plus closing costs (perhaps another $5,000 to $7,000) to make the deal. In today's marketplace, not too many buyers have that much cash.

Thus, after a period of having your house on the market, you may decide that you have to do something to convert those would-be buyers to real buyers. That something is helping them with the down payment. If, for example, you gave them a loan for part of the down payment, they wouldn't have to come up with so much cash. That might facilitate a sale. If you were flexible, you might be able to sell your property more quickly.

If you decide to do just that, to assist the buyer in financing, just what are you getting yourself in for?

The Second Mortgage

The most common form of seller-assisted financing is the *second mortgage.* Here, instead of getting all cash, you take back a mortgage for a portion of the sales price. For example, the buyers may have 10 percent cash to put down but can qualify only for an 80 percent mortgage, so you carry the remaining balance for 10 percent.

80% institutional mortgage	10% second mortgage	10% cash

There may be some advantages for you here. For example, you may get a relatively high interest rate, compared with sticking the same money in the bank. The bank may pay only 4 percent, but the second mortgage might be for 9 or 10 percent. That could mean a big return.

On the other hand, there are disadvantages. If the buyer defaults for any reason and doesn't make the payments, your only recourse might be to foreclose on your second mortgage and take the property back.

This can be an expensive proposition. The foreclosure process, depending on your state, can take months up to almost a year. There probably will be back payments on the first mortgage to make up during that time, plus taxes, insurance and the costs of foreclosure. In addition, once you get the property back, it may be in terrible shape and require a major fix-up.

My own feeling with regard to second mortgages is that if I help the buyer by providing one, I don't count it as money gained. Rather, I just forget about it. If the buyer pays regularly and eventually pays off, I regard it as a boon. If the buyer doesn't make payments, I then have to decide whether or not it's worthwhile to foreclose. In some cases, I have simply forgotten the debt because the costs of foreclosure were too great. (Of course, in those cases I was able to sell for a high enough price that the second mortgage was gravy.) In other cases, foreclosure made sense. Prices had appreciated, the property came back and after reselling, there was more profit to be made.

You must make a similar decision. If you're being asked to offer seller-assisted financing in the form of a second mortgage, you must decide whether the risk is worthwhile to you. If you are getting a high enough price, or if you're desperate to sell, you may go along with seller financing. My suggestion, however, is that you don't think of it as money in the bank. The world of second mortgages is fraught with problems and pitfalls.

To help you estimate the actual risk involved, consider the chart in Figure 10.5. It is based on the rule:

 Rule for Second Mortgage Risk

The more the buyer puts down in cash, the safer your second mortgage.

Nothing-Down Offers

When you sell FSBO, you can expect to get all kinds of offers, many of which may be totally wacky, but unless you are careful, you may not recognize the bad offers from the good. One of the most common offers you are likely to receive is the offer of no down payment at all.

Here the buyers will not only offer you nothing down but may also want you to pay all of the closing costs. As an enticement, these buyers may offer you full price.

The seller who accepts such a nothing-down offer is usually one who is blinded by price and overlooks the reality of the deal. Buyers who put no cash into a deal have no strong commitment to make monthly payments or to keep up the property. Such buyers may simply be out to resell for a profit as soon as possible.

FIGURE 10.5   Level of Risk of Second Mortgage for Seller

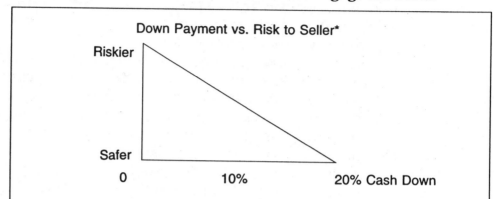

*Note: Sometimes the buyers will put down a seemingly large down payment, but will then want you to pay the closing costs. Figure 10.5 is based on the assumption that buyers not only put up a substantial down, but also pay their own closing costs. If you must pay their closing costs, that's far less money for you out of the deal.

If the market is going up and they are able to resell, you could come out okay, but in recent years the housing markets in most parts of the country have been quite bad. If your buyers find that in tough times they can't easily rent out the property for the payments, they may just walk, that is, abandon the property.

Yes, this may taint their credit history, but some people may not care, and in any event, you would be stuck with trying to foreclose to get the property back. Now, not only would you have all the foreclosure costs mentioned earlier, but no cash down in your pocket to help alleviate them.

To my way of thinking, selling for no down payment is just asking for trouble. You are, in effect, delaying your current problem and making it worse. Your current problem is selling your home. By selling nothing down, you turn that problem over to someone else who really doesn't care about you and who might dump the whole thing back in your lap in a few months, only with far more costs and expenses for you to bear.

Other Forms of Seller Financing

The second mortgage, although it is the most common form of seller financing, is not the only kind. If you own the property free and clear and if you want a steady income at an interest rate far higher than you could secure through a bank, CD or other similar device, you might want to handle all the financing yourself by giving the buyer a first mortgage.

If you decide to offer a first, be sure that you go through the procedures a normal lender would. Insist on a credit report, verify income and be sure buyers put down at least 10 percent plus closing costs in cash.

Wraps

Another form of seller-assisted financing is called the *wrap*. Here, you keep the existing first mortgage on your property yourself and the buyers pay you a single mortgage payment that includes the first and your second. In turn, you make the payments on the first and keep the balance for yourself. The wrap is fairly common in commercial deals where it is done with the consent of the lender. In residential deals, however, the lender is often not told. In fact, the whole point may be to circumvent the due-on-sale clause in the first mortgage, which specifically prohibits wraps.

Many sellers are tempted by the wrap, particularly because it seems that they have greater control. They know when the payments are being made on the existing first mortgage. Further, it may be the only offer they've recently received on their property.

The problem with the wrap, as noted above, is that it usually breaks the terms of your first mortgage and puts you in jeopardy of foreclosure. Most first mortgages today require you to pay them off in full, if and when you sell the property. By wrapping around the first, you don't tell the lender of the sale and hope to continue making the payments and to keep the mortgage.

However, as soon as you record the sale, notice is given to the lender of the first mortgage. Many times sellers hope and pray that the lender of the first simply doesn't pick up the notice of sale. (Many times the lender won't!)

The risk, however, is that if the lender does, you could find yourself being foreclosed upon and could ultimately lose all of your interest in the property. (Your alternative would be to negotiate with the lender, or to get a new loan—something quite difficult if you've already sold your house to someone else!)

To avoid this, sellers sometimes won't want to record the sale. If you do this, chances are that the lender will never find out you've sold the property. However, the buyer has no real protection that you won't resell it to someone else. Hence, most buyers will insist on recordation.

If wraps seem confusing and dangerous, it's because they are. Unless you have really sound advice to the contrary from your personal real estate adviser, I'd suggest that you *stay away from wraps.*

Lease/Option

Here, instead of selling, you rent out your home to a potential buyer on a long-term lease, usually a couple of years. The buyer often pays a higher rent with a portion of it to be applied in the future to a down payment. The buyer has the option of eventually purchasing the property. You can often get the majority of your money out by refinancing on your own before lease/optioning.

If you get a lot of option money up front, say 5 percent of the ultimate purchase price, if the buyer continues to make payments on time and if the buyer eventually purchases, the lease/ option can be an excellent method of selling a property.

However, too often the tenant/buyer doesn't want to put up much option money, perhaps none. Too often the tenant/buyer, after perhaps half the term of the lease, discovers he or she won't really be able to buy, and begins paying late, lets the property go and eventually abandons it. Sometimes, in the worst case, the tenant/buyer won't pay and won't leave and you have to initiate eviction proceedings. Eviction, however, is made more difficult because the option, at least in theory, gives the tenant/buyer some slight ownership interest in the property. It could take you longer and it could be more expensive to evict under a lease/option than under a standard lease.

I have had arguments with other real estate professionals who are proponents of lease/options. They always seem able to point to cases where it has worked out beautifully. I, on the other hand, have seen too many cases where it has not.

My suggestion is to be very careful with the lease/option and remember that it's not a sale. It's converting your home-for-sale to a rental with a hoped-for sale sometime in the future.

 ### The Best Rule I Have Found

Never assist with financing unless the buyer agrees to an arm's-length purchase, puts at least 10 percent down and pays, in cash, for the majority of the closing costs. You might lose some sales by insisting on this. But the ones you make are more likely to stick.

CHAPTER

ELEVEN

Tax Planning for FSBOs

The decision to sell is sometimes made for us. Perhaps there's a change in the location of our job or maybe there's a divorce or death, or something else occurs which makes it imperative that we sell our home. Sometimes there's nothing we can do; we just have to sell.

Most of the time, however, we *do* have choices, and the biggest choice we have is timing. We can choose to sell now or to sell later. (Of course, we can also choose how we sell—outright, trade or installment—but those aren't usually as big a consideration with homeowners.)

Choosing when to sell can make a huge difference in terms of how we come out of the deal with regard to taxes. Sell today and perhaps pay a third of your profit in taxes. Sell next month and maybe pay no taxes immediately! Yes, it is possible that timing could be that critical.

In this chapter we're going to get a brief overview of how taxes affect the sale of our home. We're also going to look at some questions about tax planning that every person selling as a FSBO should consider.

Caution

Before we begin, however, a word of caution. The tax rules are constantly reinterpreted and occasionally changed. Further, it is not possible to explain in detail all of the possible ramifications of tax law in a short chapter such as this. Therefore, the following material should be considered as simply an overview. You should not rely on it for your own tax preparation. Neither the author nor the publisher is in the business of providing tax advice. For tax advice consult with your own competent tax professional such as a Certified Public Accountant or tax attorney.

The Rollover Rule

Probably the biggest tax break that the average citizen has available is the rollover rule for a home. This means that, providing you follow the rules, you can buy your home, sell for a profit and then, instead of paying taxes on that profit as you would expect, "roll it over" into another home. In other words, instead of paying taxes and giving up some of your profits, you plow them *all* into the next home.

No, the profit isn't forgiven, but you don't pay it now, and, if you keep repeating the procedure, maybe you never pay it. Here's how it works. Let's say you sell your house and have a taxable gain of $100,000. As the current tax code stands, you'd add that to your taxes and pay up to a federal maximum capital gains rate.

With the rollover, you go out and buy another home, meeting certain guidelines, and then you don't have to pay tax on your gain immediately. You don't even have to invest the gain in the new property!

You can continue to do this time and again, rolling over the profit each time. Eventually, when you die, your heirs may end up inheriting the property at its then current value. (Technically, they may not have to pay gain on the inheritance, but if this is something you're concerned about, see a good tax attorney.)

The rule is about deferral. That means putting off into the future what you would otherwise owe today. Any gain (loosely defined as profit) you make on the sale of your home is deferred forward.

Generally, you can use the deferral rule on your taxable gain on the sale of your home provided that you meet at least three very strict rules:

1. The first is that the house must be your principal residence.
2. The second is that you must buy another personal residence within four years. (Two years before or two years after the sale of your old residence.)
3. The new residence must be for an equal or greater amount than you sold your former residence in order to claim a full rollover.

What Is a Principal Residence?

In order to qualify for the deferral, the property must be your principal residence. The government gives a lot of leeway as to what that means. Your principal residence can be your house, condo or other type of home. A trailer home has been considered a personal residence, as has a house boat!

It's important to understand, however, what principal residence really means. It has to be where you reside most of the time. (A vacation home that you visit only occasionally won't fit the bill.) It has to be truly your home.

A lot of confusion occurs with regard to rentals. Can a rental be a personal residence? Obviously if you're the tenant, the answer is "no," but, what if you're the landlord?

Let's say that you own a duplex (or duet as it's called in some parts of the country). It consists of two units: you live in one side while you rent the other out. Is the duplex your principal residence?

Yes and no. Strictly speaking, only half of it is. The part in which you reside is your principal residence. The part that you rent out is investment property.

For purposes of the deferral rule, the part in which you reside is your residence, therefore, half of any gain should be subject to deferral, while the part of the gain coming from the rental side should be subject to capital gains taxes in the year the property is sold.

Note: As mentioned above, the term *capital gains taxes* currently means that you add your gain onto your regular income and pay up to the maximum capital gains tax on it. That's a substantial amount of tax but could be significantly less than the highest tax brackets for individuals.

What happens if, after living in your home for many years, you move and rent it out. Later you decide to sell. Is it still your principal residence? Let's take an example. Say that you have lived in your home for eight years. Now you're transferred to another city and you can't sell the house, so you lease it out and move.

A year later your tenant moves out and you decide to sell. You move back in on the weekends and attempt to sell it FSBO. Within three months it sells and you have a gain of $50,000. Is the house your principal residence on which you can defer your gain? Or, is it investment property on which you must pay tax in the year of sale because you were renting it out and it became investment property?

Unfortunately, there is no absolute rule here, although some tax consultants would argue that if you have rented out your property for two years or less, it can still be construed as your principal residence. In other words, you can move, rent it out and then sell it within two years without even moving back and probably still successfully claim the deferral. You probably could even have taken depreciation on the property during the rental period!

Living in the Home before Selling

A common problem occurs when you've moved out and rented the property for a much longer period of time. For example, what if you haven't lived there, but rented it out, for three years or four? Can you still claim it as your principal residence?

As we all know, anything can be claimed, but, I suspect that the Internal Revenue Service isn't likely to look favorably on such a claim. If you have rented the property out for more than two years, it is most likely that you will be challenged as to whether or not it's your principal residence.

However, there may still be a way. One couple I know had rented out their home for six years and then planned to sell it. They wanted to claim it as their principal residence, so they went to their accountant for advice. He told them, "No way." They hadn't lived in the house for six years, had rented it out during that period and had depreciated it during that time. It definitely was investment property and wasn't their principal residence anymore.

So, the couple moved back in and reestablished the home as their principal residence. They lived in the property for about nine months and then sold it. They claimed that because they had moved back in and lived there for about a year, it was now their principal residence. Their accountant agreed with them.

Can you plan ahead and do what this couple did? Maybe. It's a gray area in the tax law. Check with your accountant first to see if your situation qualifies.

How Quickly Must You Replace Your Home?

The second major condition of the deferral rule requires that you replace your existing principal residence with a new one within a four-year period. The date of sale of your old home is smack dab in the middle of the four years. You have two years before the date of the sale, or two years after. (It can be up to four years or more after a sale for members of the military, provided strict rules are met.)

Further, you must *occupy* the property within the two-year term. Simply buying it isn't enough. This latter provision comes especially into play when you build a new property. To qualify, the new property must be completed and you must be moved in within the two-year term.

Note that the replacement home can be purchased *before* you sell your current home. That gives you much greater leeway in finding another principal residence.

Planning Ahead

What this means is that you will want to plan on buying or building another principal residence within the two–year period before or after you sell. A great mistake that some people make is thinking that because they can defer money in the year they sell their old principal residence, they don't have to do anything more. They spend the money and then awaken three years later to find a huge tax bill plus interest and penalties.

Buying a More Expensive Home

With inflation, it's not that hard to buy a new home that costs more than your old one. In order to defer *all* of the gain on the sale of your old principal residence, the purchase price of your new one must be *greater* than the sales price of your old one.

A word of caution here. When you roll over the gain, it's important to know what that gain really is. It is, in fact, the difference between the sales price of your old home (less costs of sale), and the adjusted basis of your old home. "Adjusted basis" usually means what you paid for the place plus any improvements you've added such as the cost of a new room, minus such things as depreciation.

If this is starting to sound like a lot of legalese, be aware that calculating how much gain to roll over and determining the starting basis of your new home is fairly complex. Unless you're well versed with the arcane subject of taxation, I suggest you hire a very competent CPA or tax attorney to do it for you.

There's a special part of the rule that has to do with the price of the new home that many people overlook. If the purchase price of the new principal residence is less than the sales price of the old one, you may still be able to defer *some* of the gain. In other words, you don't lose everything if you buy a cheaper home. Some of your gain may still be deferrable while you may need to pay taxes on a portion. Again, if this is your situation, check with your tax adviser.

Multiple Replacements

Some people think that this deferral rule is so handy that they want to do it over and over again. After all, why not simply buy a home, move in, live there for six months, sell it for a profit (provided that the market allows this) and buy yet another? According to this theory, you could house hop and make a fortune along the way by deferring all your taxes.

Don't try it. You can apply the rule only *once every two years.* If you try doing it sooner than two years, you will end up paying taxes on your gain from one or more of your transactions. (There are exceptions to the rule. For example, you may be able to have more than one rollover every two years if you are forced to move by an employer.)

Plan ahead. Plan to stay in your principal residence for at least two years.

Rental versus Residence

Although it seems fairly straightforward, another confusion has to do with rental property. Many people think that when we say *principal residence* the term is synonymous with *residential property,* as opposed, for example, to commercial property. Thus, if they own a house that they are renting out, they think that they can put up a FSBO sign on it, sell it and defer the gain.

Remember, we are talking about only one kind of home here—your principal residence. You can have only one principal residence at a time. A rental property does not qualify except as noted above.

A Boon When You Reach 55

When you reach the age of 55 you qualify for another big tax break. It's called the once-in-a-lifetime exclusion.

When you sell your principal residence, it allows you to exclude up to $125,000 of your gain, permanently, from your taxes. You don't have to pay taxes on it, ever.

The idea here was to provide a way out for taxpayers who were nearing retirement age and who had most of their assets in their home. They could sell, then buy a cheaper home and keep up to $125,000 for living or other expenses without paying taxes on it.

Rules for the Exclusion

To qualify for the $125,000 exclusion you must meet certain strict rules. The basic rules include the following:

- You must be 55 or older on the date of the sale.
- You must have lived in the home (and owned it) for at least the past three out of five years ending with the date of sale.
- Neither you nor your spouse may have previously taken the exemption.

While these rules may seem simple, their interpretation can be quite complex. If you're over 55 or will be when you sell, I definitely suggest that you consult with your tax adviser to see if you qualify.

By the way, it's important to understand that the exclusion is available only once in a lifetime. You can't take it again and again. If you've done it once, that's it.

Planning Ahead

Timing your sale, as I noted at the onset, is everything. If you or your spouse are nearing the age of 55, you may want to postpone selling for awhile. For example, if you're 54, you may want to hold off on the sale until the next year. By doing so you may be able to take advantage of the exclusion.

On the other hand, you also have to consider the market. Markets are sometimes depressed, sometimes active. The real estate markets in most areas of the country have largely recovered from the recent real estate recession as of this writing. If the market in your area is currently up, you may want to sell immediately to take advantage of it. Waiting could mean the market might reverse again, it would take a longer time to sell and you would get a lower price. These disadvantages might outweigh the advantages to be obtained from the over–55 rule.

Combining the Rollover with the Over-55 Rule

If you qualify for the over-55 exclusion noted above, you can combine it with the deferral rule described earlier. For example, let's say that you live in a high-priced area, you sell your home and your gain is $225,000.

You can exclude $125,000 of the gain under the over-55 rule. You can then buy a lower-priced home and defer the remaining gain using the deferral rule described earlier. In other words, you can have your cake and eat it, too. Check with your tax adviser to see if you qualify and how to handle the specifics of the transactions *before* you put your home up for sale.

Checklist

To help you plan ahead for the tax consequences of the sale of your home, you may want to use the tax-planning checklist in Figure 11.1. It leads you through the points you need to consider regarding the advantages that may be available to you. I also

FIGURE 11.1

☑ **FSBO Tax-Planning Checklist**

1. Is my house my personal residence?   Yes _____   No _____

2. Has it been more than two years since it was my personal residence?   Yes _____   No _____

3. Can I convert it to my personal residence?   Yes _____   No _____

4. Is a portion of the property not my personal residence?   Yes _____   No _____

5. What about a home office?   Yes _____   No _____

6. Will I have to pay taxes on that portion?   Yes _____   No _____

7. Am I or is my spouse over 55 years of age?   Yes _____   No _____

8. Do I meet the qualifications for the $125,000 exclusion? (Check with your tax adviser.)   Yes _____   No _____

9. Can I buy a lower-priced home and combine the exclusion with the deferral to avoid paying taxes?   Yes _____   No _____

10. Should I wait until I or my spouse is 55 to take advantage of the deferral?   Yes _____   No _____

suggest looking into, *Tips & Traps for Saving on All Your Real Estate Taxes,* with co-author Norman Lane, McGraw-Hill, 1994.

CHAPTER
TWELVE

The Disclosure Statement

One of the most significant changes occurring in real estate has to do with seller's liability. Just a few years ago the rule was "buyer beware." It was up to the buyer to determine any defects in the property. You, as a seller, could sit back smugly and sell a pig in a poke, knowing that you were unlikely to have repercussions.

That's not so anymore. Litigation in many states has led to the concept that the seller has a duty to inform buyers of any known (and many unknown!) defects in the property. If you, as a seller, don't disclose the problems with the property, when you sell, it's possible, even likely, that the buyers could come back later on and claim to have been deceived. They could even sue for damages and, conceivably, for rescission (which means that you would have to take the house back!).

While these dire consequences are unlikely, they have happened. I personally know of several cases in which buyers sued sellers over undisclosed defects. The buyers won each time.

As a result of disclosure concerns, many states have instituted compulsory disclosure laws. Sellers in those states *must* disclose defects upon sale. Most other states are currently looking into such laws. There's a chance that by the time you sell your property, you will fall under disclosure regulations.

In this chapter we're going to look at disclosure from two perspectives. The first is my theory of what you should disclose. The second is how to go about doing it.

Theory of Disclosure

The way I see it, disclosure actually protects the seller more than the buyer. If you disclose a defect and the buyer moves ahead with the purchase knowing that the defect exists, you should be free and clear. Perhaps an example will help.

I recently sold a property where there were significant cracks in the slab. (In some parts of the country, a house is built atop a slab of concrete that is poured on top of the ground; there is no basement or crawl area whatsoever underneath.) When slabs crack, it means that there may be many occasional resulting cracks in the walls and ceilings as well. In a severe case, the floor could split with one spot being higher than another. It can be a bad problem and a buyer who purchased a home unaware such a defect existed could be angry enough to seek redress.

Therefore, I gave the buyer a disclosure statement (described later on) on which I noted that there were cracks in the slab, making it unstable, particularly in wet weather. I also noted there were cracks in the walls and in the ceilings. In short, I gave the buyer every notice possible of the defect. Further, I suggested that the buyer should hire his own inspector to come in and check out the problems, which he did. The inspector noted the cracks as well but indicated they were old and unlikely to cause further trouble.

The house was sold and everything seemed fine until later that winter when the area had an abnormally large amount of rain. The ground became soaked and expanded, as can be the case with clay soils. The old cracks became larger and new ones appeared in the ceilings and walls. The furious buyer called wanting me to fix all the problems.

I tried to calm him down, then reminded him that I had informed him of the cracks in the slab and in the walls and ceilings. He said he didn't care; he didn't realize what could happen and that if I didn't make the repairs he would hire an attorney.

I told him that an attorney was a good idea and to ask one what his chances of recovery were. We ended the conversation on that note. It's been several years and I haven't heard from that buyer since.

The moral here is that I believe it's best to disclose everything. I have become known among associates as one who provides incredible disclosure statements. My disclosures are extensive and detailed.

And why not? Most sellers erroneously fear that disclosing defects will cause the buyer to shy away. I have found that not to be the case. Most buyers who are sincerely interested in the property will accept defects, or will negotiate the price to compensate for them, or will work with the seller to correct them. More to the point, the property is what it is. If it has a defect, it's better that you get it out in the open than that the buyer discover it a few months later.

Unknown Defects

Changes in disclosure requirements have an added twist that would be comical if it weren't so serious. As a seller, you may be required to disclose defects in your home that even you don't know about! For example, you could have a bad gas line leading to your hot water heater. You may not know about it, but if you fail to disclose it and later on, after a sale, there is a gas explosion in the property, you might be held responsible.

Incredible? The theory here is that as a seller it is up to you to investigate and discover most problems, certainly those involving health and safety, that occur with your property and correct them as well as reveal them to the buyer. In other words, to protect yourself, you should have a competent inspector look over the property before the sale to determine if there are hidden problems. Presumably, if the inspector gives you a clean bill of health, you're okay.

(Note: Most inspectors are great, but a few aren't. To protect themselves against complaints, many inspectors today will include their own disclosure statement in their reports saying they are not responsible for anything they don't find and, in some cases, even for things they do find! For more information, I suggest you look into my book *The Home Inspection Troubleshooter*, Real Estate Education Company, 1994.)

Of course, this means that it's to your advantage to have an inspector check over your house. If anything happens later on, you can always point to the inspection and say that you made a good effort to determine any problems.

However, you probably won't have to pay for that inspection. Agents have worked hard to convince buyers that they need the inspection to uncover hidden defects that you, the seller, haven't disclosed. Therefore, most buyers are already primed to pay for an inspection. All you have to do is recommend it and nine out of ten buyers are ready to pay for it. In reality they are paying, in part, to relieve you of potential liability.

Uncovered Defects

There's always the problem of defects that either you disclose or that the inspection uncovers and to which the buyer objects. For example, the inspection reveals that you don't have ground fault interrupter (GFI) plugs in your bathroom, which your local building code currently requires. (GFI plugs help prevent electric shock but weren't required by most building codes until fairly recently.) Or, the inspector notes that virtually all of the screens on your house's windows are old, decaying and should be replaced.

If it were my house, I would immediately replace the plugs with new GFI outlets. It's a matter of health and safety and it's simply a cost that I have to bear. (They cost only about $10 apiece.)

On the other hand, screens are negotiable. The buyer wants me to replace the screens because it was in the inspection report, but I want a few extra days in which to move out. We compromise. I get my extra days; the buyer gets new screens.

When it comes to issues that don't involve health and safety, but that are negotiable, discuss them with the buyer. In most circumstances you can reach a compromise.

By the way, money is a great compromiser. I was recently selling another home, and a termite inspection revealed that a very large back deck was ruined by dry rot. The buyer wanted it replaced, at a cost of about $3,500 to me. Instead I offered the buyer a reduction in price of $2,000 and acceptance of the deck as is. I pointed out that he could have the cash now, and later on as he had the opportunity, he could use the money to buy decking and rebuild the deck himself. He was quite happy with this arrangement.

Methods of Disclosure

The simplest method of disclosure is to tell buyers about a problem as you show them the property. As you walk by the fireplace, for example, you note that it has a crack in the flue. The estimated cost of repair is $1,500. You're prepared to take that off the price.

What you have to be particularly careful of, however, is documenting the disclosure. Yes, you may have fully explained the problem to the buyers, but six months later, when they claim you never told them, what do you have to back it up? If you have a disclosure statement describing the problem with their signatures on it, you're in much better shape.

When To Provide a Written Disclosure Statement

The actual disclosure statement will vary enormously from area to area. In some parts of the country, no official disclosure statement exists, and you will want to have your attorney draw it up for you. Figure 12.1 is an example of a typical disclosure statement. The question arises, however, of whether you should disclose all defects to the buyer up front or whether you should wait and disclose them after the buyer has signed an agreement.

In California, which has some of the toughest disclosure laws in the country, a seller may give the buyer a written disclosure statement after the deal has been signed. However, the buyer then has three full days to rescind the deal with no penalty (no loss of deposit) for any reason.

In buying property some shrewd buyers have taken advantage of this California state law to make deals and then continue shopping around, knowing they have a full three days to back out without penalty. As a consequence, wise sellers give the disclosure statement to the buyer as soon as the deal is made. (Note: You want the buyer to sign an acknowledgment that he or she has actually received the statement.)

The Disclosure Statement

As noted, the disclosure statement can take a wide variety of forms. Figure 12.1 is an example.

FIGURE 12.1

 Sample Disclosure Statement

THE FOLLOWING STATEMENT IS NOT INTENDED TO BE USED WITHOUT
THE AID OF YOUR ATTORNEY. TAKE IT TO YOUR ATTORNEY AND ASK
HIM OR HER TO MAKE IT APPROPRIATE FOR YOUR STATE AND LOCALE
AND FOR YOUR SPECIFIC TRANSACTION.

SELLER'S DISCLOSURE STATEMENT

(To be filled out by seller and given to buyer. Seller, use a separate page to
explain any defects or problems with property.)

WATER

Any leaks (now or before) in the roof?	Yes _____	No _____
Around a skylight, at a chimney, door, window or elsewhere?	Yes _____	No _____

Was the problem corrected? _____

_____

How?_____

By whom? _____

When?_____By permit?_____Final inspection when?_____

Does the house have gutters?	Yes _____	No _____

Condition? _____

Does the house have downspouts?	Yes _____	No _____

Condition? _____

Any drainage problems?	Yes _____	No _____

Explain _____

How corrected? _____

Water directed away from house?	Yes _____	No _____

FIGURE 12.1 *(Continued)*

Flooding or grading problems?	Yes _____	No _____
Settling, slipping, sliding or other kinds of soil problems?	Yes _____	No _____
Any leaks at sinks, toilets, tubs, showers or elsewhere in house?	Yes _____	No _____
Public water?____ Or well?____	Yes _____	No _____
Date well pump installed?_____		
Low water pressure?	Yes _____	No _____

TITLE

Are you involved in a bankruptcy?	Yes _____	No _____
Are you in default on any mortgage?	Yes _____	No _____
Do you currently occupy the property?	Yes _____	No _____
Have you given anyone else an option lease or right of first refusal on the property?	Yes _____	No _____
Does the property have any bond liens?	Yes _____	No _____
Can they be paid off without penalty?	Yes _____	No _____
Are there any boundary disputes?	Yes _____	No _____
Any encroachments or easements?	Yes _____	No _____
Shared walls, fences or other such areas?	Yes _____	No _____
Any areas held in common such as pools, tennis courts, walkways, greenbelts or other?	Yes _____	No _____
Notices of abatement filed?	Yes _____	No _____
Any lawsuits against seller that will affect title?	Yes _____	No _____
Do you have a real estate license?	Yes _____	No _____
Is there a Homeowners' Association to which you must belong?	Yes _____	No _____

FIGURE 12.1 *(Continued)*

Any current lawsuits involving the   Yes _____   No _____
Homeowners' Association?

Any Conditions, Covenants and   Yes _____   No _____
Restrictions (CC&Rs) in deed affecting
property?

Any easements or rights-of-way over   Yes _____   No _____
property to public utilities or others?

STRUCTURE

Any cracks in slab?   Yes _____   No _____

Any cracks in interior walls?   Yes _____   No _____

Any cracks in ceilings?   Yes _____   No _____

Any cracks in exterior walls?   Yes _____   No _____

Any cracks in foundation?   Yes _____   No _____

Any retaining walls?   Yes _____   No _____

   Cracked?_____ Leaning?_____ Broken?_____

Any driveway cracks?   Yes _____   No _____

Any problems with fences?   Yes _____   No _____

Is house insulated?   Yes _____   No _____

   Attic?_____ Walls?_____ Floor?_____

Double-paned glass windows?   Yes _____   No _____

Moisture barrier in areas below ground   Yes _____   No _____
level?

Sump pump?   Yes _____   No _____

   Where?_____

   Why?_____

Septic tank?   Yes _____   No _____

   Active?_____ Abandoned?_____ Filled?_____

Connected to sewer?   Yes _____   No _____

FIGURE 12.1 *(Continued)*

EQUIPMENT

Central furnace?   Yes _____   No _____

    Forced air?_____ Radiant/water?_____

    Radiant/electric?_____ Other? _____

Room heaters?   Yes _____   No _____

    Type?_____

    Location? _____

Central air-conditioning?   Yes _____   No _____

    Installed date? _____

Room air-conditioners?   Yes _____   No _____

    Location? _____

Furnace room vented?   Yes _____   No _____

Temperature relief valve on water heater?   Yes _____   No _____

Spa?   Yes _____   No _____

Pool?   Yes _____   No _____

    Pool heated?   Yes _____   No _____

    Cracks, leaks or other problems with   Yes _____   No _____
    pool?

    Explain _____

Any aluminum wiring?   Yes _____   No _____

HAZARDS AND VIOLATIONS

Any asbestos?   Yes _____   No _____

Any environmental hazards including, but   Yes _____   No _____
not limited to, radon gas, lead-based paint,
storage tanks for diesel or other fuel,
contaminants in soil or water,
formaldehyde?

Landfill on or near property?   Yes _____   No _____

Is property in earthquake zone?   Yes _____   No _____

FIGURE 12.1 *(Continued)*

Is property in flood-hazard zone?	Yes _____	No _____
Is property in landslide area?	Yes _____	No _____
Is property in high fire-hazard area as described on a Federal Emergency Management Agency Flood Insurance Rate Map or Flood Hazard Boundary Map?	Yes _____	No _____
Is property in any special study zone that indicates a hazard or requires permission to add to or alter existing structure?	Yes _____	No _____
Are there any zoning violations pertaining to property? (Explain separately.)	Yes _____	No _____
Were any room additions built without appropriate permits? (Explain separately.)	Yes _____	No _____
Was any work done to electrical, plumbing, gas or other home systems without appropriate permit? (Explain separately.)	Yes _____	No _____
Does the property have an energy conservation retrofit?	Yes _____	No _____
Any odors caused by gas, toxic waste, agriculture or other?	Yes _____	No _____
Were pets kept on the property?	Yes _____	No _____
Type?_____ Inside?_____		
Are there any pet odor problems?	Yes _____	No _____
Are there any active springs on property?	Yes _____	No _____
Any sinkholes on property?	Yes _____	No _____

FIGURE 12.1 *(Continued)*

Is property adjacent to or near any existing or planned mining sites, toxic waste sites or other environmental hazards?	Yes _____	No _____
Is there any real estate development planned or pending in immediate area such as commercial, industrial or residential development that could affect property values?	Yes _____	No _____
Any abandoned septic tank?	Yes _____	No _____
Is a Home Protection Plan available to the buyer?	Yes _____	No _____

REPORTS THAT HAVE BEEN MADE

The seller Notes that the following reports have been made and are available to the buyer:

Structural	Yes _____	No _____
Geologic	Yes _____	No _____
Roof	Yes _____	No _____
Soil	Yes _____	No _____
Sewer/septic	Yes _____	No _____
Heating/air-conditioning	Yes _____	No _____
Electrical/plumbing	Yes _____	No _____
Termite	Yes _____	No _____
Pool/spa	Yes _____	No _____
General home inspection	Yes _____	No _____
Energy audit	Yes _____	No _____
Radon test	Yes _____	No _____
City inspection	Yes _____	No _____

FIGURE 12.1 *(Continued)*

ITEMS THAT GO WITH THE PROPERTY

Window coverings	Yes _____	No _____
Floor coverings	Yes _____	No _____
Range	Yes _____	No _____
Oven	Yes _____	No _____
Microwave	Yes _____	No _____
Dishwasher	Yes _____	No _____
Trash compactor	Yes _____	No _____
Garbage disposal	Yes _____	No _____
Bottled water	Yes _____	No _____
Burglar alarm system	Yes _____	No _____
Gutters	Yes _____	No _____
Fire alarm	Yes _____	No _____
Intercom	Yes _____	No _____
Electric washer/dryer hookups	Yes _____	No _____
Sauna	Yes _____	No _____
Hot tub	Yes _____	No _____
Spa	Yes _____	No _____
Pool	Yes _____	No _____
Central heating	Yes _____	No _____
Central air	Yes _____	No _____
Central evaporative cooler	Yes _____	No _____
Water softener	Yes _____	No _____
Space heaters	Yes _____	No _____
Solar heating	Yes _____	No _____
Window air-conditioners	Yes _____	No _____
Sprinklers	Yes _____	No _____

Where? _____

FIGURE 12.1 *(Continued)*

Security gates	Yes _____	No _____
Television antenna	Yes _____	No _____
TV cable connections	Yes _____	No _____
TV satellite dish	Yes _____	No _____
Attached garage	Yes _____	No _____
Detached garage	Yes _____	No _____
Water heater	Yes _____	No _____

    Gas _____ Electric _____

City water supply	Yes _____	No _____
Public utility gas	Yes _____	No _____
Propane gas	Yes _____	No _____
Screens on windows	Yes _____	No _____
Sump pump	Yes _____	No _____
Built-in barbecue	Yes _____	No _____
Garage door opener	Yes _____	No _____

    Number of remote controls _____

Is the property equipped with smoke detectors?	Yes _____	No _____

ITEMS THAT ARE SPECIFICALLY EXCLUDED FROM THE SALE

Lamps _____ Where?_____

Window coverings _____ Where? _____

Other Items   Yes _____   No _____

Explain _____

_____

FIGURE 12.1 *(Continued)*

SELLER IS AWARE OF THE FOLLOWING DEFECTS AND/OR
MALFUNCTIONS AND SPECIFICALLY DRAWS BUYER'S ATTENTION TO
THEM:

_____

_____

_____

_____

BUYER IS ENCOURAGED TO MAKE A PHYSICAL INSPECTION OF THE
PROPERTY AND TO EMPLOY THE SERVICES OF A COMPETENT
INSPECTION COMPANY TO OBTAIN AN INDEPENDENT VERBAL AND
WRITTEN REPORT OF THE PROPERTY'S CONDITION.

SIGNED BY SELLER AND BUYER

_____

_____

CHAPTER THIRTEEN

The Closing

There are two kinds of closing. One is closing the deal, which we've spoken about already in several earlier chapters, notably 7 and 8. The other type of closing is real estate jargon for jumping through all the hoops placed in front of you, so that eventually the buyers get title and you get your money out.

Unfortunately, most FSBO sellers don't worry much about this second type of closing, believing instead that it's over once the sales agreement is signed with the buyers. In truth, that may just be the beginning.

Steps in the Closing Process

Once you've found a buyer and gotten a signed sales agreement, it will normally take anywhere from a short 30 days to a long 90 days to close the deal. Along the way there are a lot of problems to solve and tasks to perform, by you. (See Figure 13.1.)

FIGURE 13.1   Steps in the Closing Process (Short 30-Day Escrow)

First Week	• Sales agreement is signed. • Buyer applies for mortgage. • Escrow is opened and deposit inserted.
Second Week	• Preliminary letter of qualification sent by lender. • Title search is completed. • Inspections are ordered.
Third Week	• Termite work and other repairs are done. • Title problems (if any) are cleared. • Lender gives buyer loan approval.
Fourth Week	• Buyer does final walk-through. • Buyer signs loan documents. • Seller signs off title. • Deal closes.

First Week

If you were working through an agent, that person would now do the grit work, those unexciting but absolutely necessary jobs that must be done. These include the following:

Be Sure That the Buyer Applies for a Mortgage. I always list this first because without a mortgage, you won't have a deal. (You have a better chance of winning a state lottery than of finding an all-cash buyer.) Although you can't normally walk the buyers to a lender, you can insert a clause in the sales agreement specifying that the buyers will immediately apply for a mortgage and the lender will provide a letter of preliminary approval within a reasonable amount of time, say seven days from the signing of the sales agreement.

You can check by phone with the buyers to find out which lender they have gone through (see Chapter 10 on financing) and then check with that lender to see how the mortgage is progressing. However, your safety valve is that preliminary letter of qualifying. If you don't get it within seven days, you may want to return the buyers' deposit and start looking for a new buyer.

The reason for being strict here is that in 99 cases out of a hundred, what makes the deal go through (title changes hands and you get your money) is having buyers who can get the necessary mortgage. In most cases, by the time you sign the sales agreement, you have been told by the buyers that they have the cash for the down payment, good credit and sufficient income to get a mortgage.

Unfortunately, you really don't know for sure. I have worked with buyers who, seemingly, had excellent credit only to find weeks into the deal that they had hidden a foreclosure or a bankruptcy or bad payments in another state. In one case a buyer told me of the enormous income he had; only later did I discover that he had to make huge alimony and child-support payments, which reduced the amount of his income that could be applied to the mortgage and disqualified him.

As soon as your buyers fill out a complete mortgage application and deliver it to the lender along with about $35 for a credit report, the lender will examine the application and call for a preliminary credit check. If the loan applicants' credit checks out and they appear to have sufficient income and cash to make the deal, the lender will normally issue the preliminary letter of qualification.

Don't take this letter to the bank. It's merely a statement of opinion and nothing more, but at least it lets you know that there's a good chance that your buyers will qualify for the needed mortgage.

Open Escrow. Most states now use escrow services for real estate transactions. These can be handled by an independent escrow company, an agent or an attorney, especially in those states where attorneys handle the closings. Opening the escrow means that you take your signed sales agreement to the escrow officer and receive an escrow number. The escrow company, in conjunction with a title insurance company, now begins a title search to be sure that you can give the buyer clear title to your property. The escrow company also will draw up all the documents (with the exception of the loan documents, which will come from the lender) needed to complete the transaction. Since this all takes time, you want to immediately open escrow after signing the sales agreement.

Also, you will want to put the deposit money the buyer gave you into escrow. As noted in Chapter 5, the buyer is unlikely to trust you with this money. The easiest solution to this potential problem is to have the check made out to escrow, an independent third party. Keep in mind, however, that if the deal doesn't go through and there is no language specifying what is to happen to the deposit in that event (see your attorney), the money will remain in escrow. It will go to neither you nor the buyer until you agree on its disposition. (I've seen a deposit languish for months in escrow while the buyer and seller argued over who was to get what. It's best that you have your attorney handle this before-hand.)

Second Week

By now the preliminary letter of the buyer's qualification should have been issued. If it hasn't, you need to find out why not. It might turn out that your buyer can't qualify.

If the letter has been issued, don't think you're home free, particularly with regard to credit. One would think that it's easy to determine creditworthiness, but it can be difficult. In the case of credit, a local credit-reporting agency may not pick up bad credit, particularly if it occurred out-of-state. On the other hand, before the lender will fund, it almost always requires a *triple credit report*. This special report is compiled from the three biggest national credit-reporting agencies. Sometimes, at the last minute, a credit blemish will turn up on one report that doesn't show on any of the others and the loan could be turned down. A letter of qualification is a good first step, but it's not a guarantee.

Get the Preliminary Title Report. This should be issued by
the second week. It will show you any problems you may have on
your title.

Don't smirk. You may have problems there you don't even
know about. For example, someone may have filed a lien on your
property in error. You may be totally innocent, but now you have
to locate whoever filed that lien, convince him or her of the error
and have this party remove it. Sometimes you have to get an attorney to accomplish this.

Other problems could affect the title, such as an encumbrance or easement that prevents you from getting clear title. It's
up to you to identify the problem and solve it.

Order Inspections. Another matter is the various inspections
that may be needed. Almost certainly the lender will require a termite clearance before funding the loan. To get this, you need to
order a termite inspection. Also, the buyer may want a housing
inspection, roofing inspection or any of a dozen other kinds of
inspections. (See previous chapters on disclosures.)

You must order these inspections. Normally the escrow
officer won't do that, although if the inspection companies agree,
you can have the bills for the inspections sent to escrow for payment.

Note: If for some reason the sale doesn't close, either you, the
buyer or both will be responsible for paying for the costs of all
inspections. That is why I suggest waiting a week to see if the
buyer gets that preliminary letter of qualification. At least now
you have a better hope that the deal will close.

Third Week

By now you should be really rolling. The inspections should
have been done and required repairs noted. In addition, after
about 21 days the lender (if it isn't too busy) should have completed all credit searches and all income and cash verifications.
When this happens the lender will now issue a final loan approval
and set a date for funding the loan. This means that your buyer

has the mortgage in the bag. (But be careful, as we'll see shortly: that bag could still have a few holes in it.)

Once the buyer has final loan approval (or earlier, as needed) you will want to authorize repair work. This may mean anything from fixing a broken window to tenting the house to remove termites. Just keep in mind that once the work is ordered, it must be paid for whether or not the deal closes, and usually you're the one to pay for it. For that reason, most sellers wait until the last possible moment before ordering the work done.

Finally, by now you should have cleared up any problems in the title. Mistaken liens and other title clouds will have been removed.

Fourth Week

By the fourth week in an ideal closing, the lender is ready to fund. The buyer may want a final walk-through. (This step must have been specified in the sales agreement or you don't have to give it, yet it's probably to your advantage to accede to avoid later problems with your buyer.) The buyer again looks at the house, mostly to see that it's in the same condition as when the sales agreement was signed.

Beware of potential problems here. Sometimes buyers will try either to get you to provide additional improvements or to wheedle out of the deal. If everyone works in good faith, it's no problem. However, if a buyer wants to be a stickler, you may find yourself beginning negotiations all over again!

Once the inspection is completed, the buyer will need to go to the escrow officer and sign all the loan documents as well as deposit the cash down payment and closing costs. The escrow officer will let you know when this has to be done. (Lenders usually leave a window of only a few days during which all the documents must be finalized.)

Once the lender has signed the documents, you will need to sign the deed as well as any additional escrow instructions.

And then you're done!

Now you wait.

You are waiting for the lender to fund the loan, then for the escrow officer to record the deed and mortgage and issue your check to you. If the deed is recorded in the morning, you can usually have your check the same day.

Problems

As the famed baseball star, Yogi Berra, was fond of saying, "It ain't over, till it's over."

What could possibly go wrong? Probably very little, but there's always something. The lender might not fund. The lender might have discovered a credit or income problem with your buyer at the 11th hour—unlikely, but it could happen—or the lender might itself suddenly be immersed in financial problems and not have the funds needed. A few years ago I would have scoffed at such an idea, but lately, with lenders becoming insolvent all around, this possibility is nothing to laugh at. Also, someone might record a lien or other encumbrance affecting your title. Again it's unlikely, but it could happen.

If the unforeseen does happen, you'll simply have to deal with it. In most cases the worst that will happen is a delay. It is possible, however, in a worst-case scenario, actually to lose the deal after everything is signed and before the deed has been recorded. I've personally never had that happen to me, but I have seen it happen to others.

Other Closings

What we've seen here is an ideal 30-day closing. Yours may take much longer. The need for extensive physical repairs may prolong the escrow, or a title problem could require an attorney and court action to eliminate, or the buyer may not be able to immediately get all the cash together, or anything else could happen. These days escrows of 60 and even 90 days are not uncommon.

Beware, however, of losing your loan in a longer-than-anticipated escrow. Lenders will often offer commitments to fund. This

FIGURE 13.2

☑ **Closing Checklist (Items You Need To Do)**

1. Be sure buyer applies for mortgage.   Done _____
2. Insist on a 7-day preliminary approval   Done _____
   letter.
3. Use signed sales agreement to open escrow   Done _____
   and place buyer's deposit in it.
4. Order inspections.   Done _____
5. Remove any title problems you may have.   Done _____
6. Check on buyer's progress in getting   Done _____
   mortgage.
7. Find out if buyer receives final loan   Done _____
   approval.
8. Order all work that needs to be done.   Done _____
9. Do final walk-through.   Done _____
10. Sign all documents.   Done _____

means that the lender guarantees a rate and points for a specified time. That time, however, is rarely more than 45 days and usually is just 30 days. If the escrow takes longer, the lender may still fund, but not at the originally quoted interest rate or points.

If interest rates have jumped up after the sales agreement was signed but before the escrow closes, it could cost your buyer more money and higher payments. He or she may not want to or be able to pay more. Depending on how the sales agreement was prepared, your buyer may be able to walk if interest rates rise above a ceiling. Or, the lender may say that your buyer qualified at a lower rate but not at the newer, higher rate.

No, it's not likely to happen, but a longer escrow can bring its own set of problems. If I have the option, I always go for the shortest escrow possible (see Figure 13.2).

CHAPTER FOURTEEN

What To Do If Your Home Doesn't Sell

What if, in spite of your best efforts, you put your house up for sale by FSBO and after a set time, say three months, it still doesn't sell? I'm sure this is a major fear in the backs of the minds of everyone considering selling FSBO.

If this happens to you, first and foremost, don't panic. It's time to get a cup of tea (or coffee), catch a deep breath and reflect. It's time to look at your alternatives. In this chapter we'll discuss what to do if your property doesn't sell.

By the way, if you're one of those anxious people who turned to this chapter first, stop. Don't bother reading here because chances are you won't need this information. Go back to the beginning, keep an optimistic outlook and get started selling your home FSBO.

FIGURE 14.1   Reasons a Home Doesn't Sell

1. Resale market is bad.

2. Location is poor.

3. Price is too high.

4. House shows badly.

5. Financing isn't competitive.

Causes

If you've given a FSBO sale your best shot and your home still hasn't sold, then you have to look for likely causes. There are five main reasons that a house doesn't sell (see Figure 14.1). Let's consider each separately.

1. Resale Market Is Bad

The residential resale market in various parts of the country began sliding as early as 1985. While, as of this writing, most areas have recovered, others still remain depressed, and a few of the recovered areas have again begun sliding downward.

While it's beyond the scope of this book to go into the reasons for the downward trend in real estate, it is worth noting that it's probably cyclical. It may repeat over and again. Therefore, I believe it's worth your while to determine the condition of the overall resale market in your area at the time you want to sell.

If you can't sell, it may simply be that nothing at all is selling. In other words, check with the local Board of REALTORS® to find out how many houses are selling per month in your area. If it's almost none, you immediately know what your problem is.

If the market in your area is severely depressed and you absolutely must sell, you really only have two alternatives. The first is to lower your price or terms until your property becomes attractive. Unfortunately, this may be down to a giveaway level. In short, you may have to give up your equity (if you have enough) in order to get rid of the property.

Bottom fishers are always looking for very low-priced houses, and one of these will undoubtedly pick up yours. (If you don't have much equity, then you may have to consider a deed in lieu of foreclosure or other means.)

The other, usually better, alternative is not to sell and wait until the market gets better. We'll consider this as an option in more detail shortly.

2. Location Is Poor

Another reason for the inability to sell is a poor location. Factors making for a poor location include the following:

- An environmental hazard such as a dump site
- High-tension electrical wires
- A sewerage facility of some sort
- A noisy or smelly factory
- A particularly high-crime area
- A blighted neighborhood
- Other factors that would alienate buyers

While you may have taken this into account initially when you bought the property, perhaps you didn't give it enough weight. Regardless of how nice your particular house is, potential buyers may be shunning your area because of some nearby detrimental influence.

If this is the case, then the only realistic thing you can do is lower your price and/or offer more advantageous terms. If you had time, you could attempt to organize the neighborhood and seek ways to change the harmful influence, but that could take years. In order to attract buyers in the short run, you may simply have to make your house into more of a bargain.

3. Price Is Too High

Even if you don't have a bad neighborhood influence, your home may still be priced too high for the local market to bear.

Perhaps you didn't do as good a job of checking comparables as you thought. Remember, while for you checking the market is an academic exercise, for buyers it is an urgent and vital task. After a few days of looking at homes, buyers become very attuned to what a house should sell for. In today's market, if your home is even a few thousand over market price, they may shun it and not make offers.

Reexamine the comparables. For a weekend, pretend you're a buyer and visit every home for sale in your area around your price range. (Work with an agent on this.) Very quickly you'll see if you've priced yourself even a little bit too high.

Then you'll have to suck in your breath and make the plunge; lower your price accordingly.

4. House Shows Badly

Reexamine the appearance of your house, only don't take *your* word on it. Seek the advice of experts. Contact two or three agents. (After having put your home up FSBO, you should have the names of dozens of agents who have contacted you.) Ask them to come in and tell them that you've had trouble selling FSBO. You're thinking of listing (which you undoubtedly are). Would they have any suggestions to make about the outside/inside presentation of your home?

You may be astonished at the suggestions offered. It may turn out that the wonderful shrubs that have lovingly grown over the years are hiding the front of your house and need to be hacked out. Maybe the entranceway that you painted lavender would look better in beige. Perhaps the tile you yourself laid in the front hall would be better if removed and a professional linoleum laid in its place.

The point here is that *you* probably aren't able to see objectively what's wrong with the presentation of your property. If two or three others, however, all agree on some item that needs to be improved, consider doing the work. Once it's done, try again to sell FSBO. Removing the objection may result in hooking a buyer.

5. Financing Isn't Competitive

Although we've discussed this, sometimes it's hard to really believe it. In a tight market, sometimes you simply cannot sell for cash. Cash-down buyers may not be out there. Hence, to get a sale, you may have to offer low-down-payment financing and carry some of the paper yourself.

I know that getting cash out of your property is often the most advantageous method of selling. You know it, too, but if your choice is to sell with paper or not to sell at all, what are you going to do? Sometimes you have to compromise.

Further, remember that a FSBO seller often has to go the extra mile to get that sale. If listed properties are getting all-cash buyers, then perhaps you have to offer to carry 5 percent paper. If listed properties are getting 10 percent cash down/10 percent paper, perhaps you will have to offer 15 percent paper. The point is that in your market, you may have to offer better terms in order to dispose of your property.

(Reread Chapter 10 on financing and be aware that carrying paper carries with it certain risks. If the buyers eventually default, you could be forced to take the property back or lose the paper.)

Other Alternatives

Let's say that you've considered the five main reasons for failure to sell and have taken what corrective steps you can and still your property doesn't sell. What are your alternatives now?

List

As noted at the beginning of this book, my suggestion is that if you do your best as a FSBO seller and you still can't find a buyer after a set period of time, then try listing. In Chapter 4 we talked about how to list for less.

Keep in mind that your goal is to sell your property. If that means listing it with an agent to accomplish that goal, then do it.

Don't find yourself wedged into a corner by stubbornness. Don't fail to sell simply because you can't do it FSBO.

The key, of course, is the time limit. As I've noted in many places, set a reasonable time limit, whether it's a couple of months or half a year. If you still have not sold after the time limit you set has expired, consider listing.

Take It off the Market

Maybe no houses are selling in your area. The market could be terrible. So terrible, in fact, that you simply can't find a buyer either FSBO or through an agent.

If that's the case, consider hanging onto your property until times get better, which they surely will. This means that you may have to hold your property for a year or more. Ideally, you will be able to continue living in your property, working in the area and making the payments. If you can do all of these, then you may simply want to defer selling for awhile. Remember, when the market eventually does turn up, you will probably be able to sell quickly and, very likely, for more money.

Lease It

Maybe you can't sell, *and* you can't stay there. Perhaps you have to move because of a change in employment. Perhaps an illness requires you to get out from under that mortgage payment. If you can't stay and you can't sell, consider leasing the property.

Very often you can lease the property for at least your mortgage payment, and you may be able to write off your interest, taxes, insurance and other costs as well as depreciation, which actually gives you a tax advantage at year end. (Note: Recent tax law changes restrict the ability to write off any real estate losses against personal income on an annual basis. Check with your accountant to see if you qualify.)

Leasing the property also carries risks. Tenants almost never treat the property as well as you would. There's bound to be some wear and tear in the best of situations and, if you get a bad tenant, there could be real damage as well as the costs of eviction.

While this can happen, if you rent judiciously it's less likely to. (I suggest you check into *The Landlord's Troubleshooter,* Real Estate Education Company, 1994.)

Lease/Option

Yet another alternative is the "lease/option." Here you lease the property to a tenant and, typically, allow a certain percentage of the higher rent payment to apply toward a down payment when he or she eventually purchases. You have combined leasing with the potential for purchase.

Lease/options become more favored during slumping real estate markets. However, their value is directly related to the tenant's eventually exercising the option and purchasing the property. If the tenant doesn't eventually buy, you will take back the property, often in poor condition because at the end of the lease/option period the tenant often resents the higher payment and takes it out on the property.

Studies have shown that the chances of the tenant's eventually buying the property improve in a direct relationship to the amount of the rent that goes to the option. For example, if the rent is $1,000 a month and $50 goes toward the option, the tenant is far less likely to buy than if $500 a month goes toward the option.

I, personally, have had mixed results with lease/options, although I do know people who have had good success. As a result, I simply cannot unconditionally recommend them.

Walking Away

In desperate situations, some sellers who can't sell (they may owe more than their property is worth), can't stay (their job may require a move to a different state) and can't lease (too many properties are for rent or for sale) simply walk away from their properties. They let the house go to foreclosure.

I don't recommend this practice, ever. A foreclosure will ruin your credit rating. Although you may be able to establish enough credit to get a credit card in a few years, it could take a decade, if ever, before a lender will give you another home mortgage.

If you are desperate, my suggestion is that you immediately call the mortgage lender to see whether it's possible to make an arrangement that would benefit both of you. Perhaps instead of foreclosure, you can simply give the lender a deed to your property. (Lenders sometimes prefer to threaten to foreclose, hoping to pressure you into keeping up your payments. Have your attorney look into the possibility of bankruptcy for you. The threat of a personal bankruptcy holding up disposition of a home for months, perhaps years, will often bring a reluctant lender around to your way of seeing things.)

Checklist for When Your House Doesn't Sell

If your house simply won't sell, go through the checklist in Figure 14.2. See if there isn't something you've overlooked.

FIGURE 14.2

Checklist for When Your House Won't Sell

1. How is the general resale market in your area? — Good ____ — Bad ____
2. If it's bad, have you tried reducing your price? — Yes ____ — No ____
3. Why not?_____
4. Do you have a bad location? — Yes ____ — No ____
5. If yes, have you tried reducing your price? — Yes ____ — No ____
6. Why not?_____
7. Have you rechecked comparables lately? — Yes ____ — No ____
8. If your house is priced above market, have you reduced price? — Yes ____ — No ____
9. Why not?_____
10. Have you asked several agents about the appearance of your home? — Yes ____ — No ____
11. If it shows badly, have you improved it? — Yes ____ — No ____
12. Why not?_____
13. Are you offering seller-financed terms? — Yes ____ — No ____
14. If not, why not?_____
15. Have you considered listing? — Yes ____ — No ____
16. Why not?_____
17. Have you considered leasing? — Yes ____ — No ____
18. What about a lease/option? — Yes ____ — No ____
19. If you're desperate, have you considered a deed in lieu of foreclosure? — Yes ____ — No ____
20. Have you talked with an attorney? — Yes ____ — No ____

Index